D1824453

Pottery and Ceramics

Pottery and Ceramics

Roger Bunn

M

© Roger Bunn 1979

All rights reserved. No part of this publication may be
reproduced or transmitted, in any form or by any
means, without permission.

First published 1979 by
THE MACMILLAN PRESS LTD
London and Basingstoke
Associated companies in Delhi Dublin
Hong Kong Johannesburg Lagos Melbourne
New York Singapore and Tokyo

Printed in Great Britain by
A. Wheaton & Co. Ltd.
Exeter.

British Library Cataloguing in Publication Data

Bunn, Roger
    Pottery and ceramics. — (Leisure learning series).
    1. Pottery craft
    I. Title II. Series
    738.1   TT920
    ISBN 0-333-27123-8
    ISBN 0-333-24062-6 Pbk

This book is sold subject to the standard conditions
of the Net Book Agreement.

The paperback edition of this book is sold subject to
the condition that it shall not, by way of trade or
otherwise, be lent, resold, hired out, or otherwise
circulated without the publisher's prior consent in
any form of binding or cover other than that in which
it is published and without a similar condition
including this condition being imposed on the
subsequent purchaser.

Contents

Preface

This book is primarily designed to give background information and assistance to people attending part-time pottery courses at further education establishments.

I have attempted to give basic information and to offer suggestions without being too directive, because as a tutor I am more interested in a student-orientated approach than a subject-orientated approach, and I prefer as soon as possible to discuss aims and ideas with individuals. Clay is a very versatile, exciting and expressive medium. It offers everyone the opportunity to realise innate creative impulses and success can be achieved at all levels.

There are many aspects of pottery on which new students need guidance; that is, if we define 'pottery' as being an entity bound within certain laws of function and necessity. For example, a handle can be good or bad. Other aspects such as wheel work require commitment and a great deal of time and practice.

But there are still other aspects, which perhaps we can call by a more general term, 'ceramics', where people can discover, experiment and create on their own terms without reference to any particular function or need. Clay is just as much an artist's medium as a craftsman-potter's medium, which is why so often in pottery both art and function go hand in hand.

The book is by no means a comprehensive gospel on studio ceramics and there is rarely only one way to do anything. However it covers the techniques in a way that follows the pattern of the ceramic process and which may well resemble many short courses. It is possible that the chapters on ideas and stimuli could well come at the beginning, and this is an approach I have used on occasions in day schools and with small groups so that the methods are discussed when and where they are relevant to particular individual needs. As a tutor I am constantly pleasantly surprised at the many different ways people, some with little previous experience, invent and interpret in clay. So, conscious that there are many excellent further education tutors with varying approaches, I have tried to avoid being dogmatic in any way, and offer this as a guide which answers some questions, poses others and suggests some avenues of exploration.

Roger Bunn

Acknowledgments

I would like to thank the following for all their help in the preparation of this book: Ron Fry, Eddie Gee and David Young for their photography; Hazel Alexander and Deborah Maughan for producing the typescript; Miss M. Macfarlane of the Hampshire Museum Service for showing me the pottery collection; Susan Stock and James Bustard of Portsmouth Museum and Art Gallery for allowing me to photograph pieces in the Gallery's collection; Harry Fraser and David Hamilton for giving permission to quote from their books; Alvin Betteridge and 'Pep' Pepper for their help and contribution; Mrs Hilda Marshall and Mrs Ida Withers for providing photographs of their pots; and, finally, Sybil for all her help and encouragement.

R. J. B.

1

Clay

Clay is a natural earth, formed millions of years ago by the weathering, erosion and decomposition of feldspathic rocks. Feldspar is a common mineral and it appears, for example, as a crystal in granite, which is an igneous rock, formed originally by the cooling of molten minerals or magmas.

There are two basic types of clay. *Primary* or *residual* clay is a pure clay which has not moved from its forming ground. This is called china clay or kaolin and it is usually *unplastic* — that is, difficult to model, and free from impurities. The molecular composition of pure clay is: alumina (Al_2O_3) 39.45 per cent, silica $(2SiO_2)$ 46.64 per cent, water $(2H_2O)$ 13.91 per cent — hence the dictionary definition of a clay as 'hydrated aluminium silicates'. The other basic type is *secondary* clay. Secondary clays are those which have become *plastic* or *malleable* through the effect of water and movement in their journey from their original forming grounds. Secondary clays contain many impurities such as metallic deposits, which may give clays colour characteristics. For example, iron gives terracotta its red colour.

CHARACTERISTICS AND PROPERTIES

The main characteristic of clay, which has made it so vastly important to man for thousands of years, is that when heated it will fuse and become permanent. It is elemental, being composed of earth and water and requiring fire to make it hard. However, not all clays are suitable for pottery. Often they are blended commercially to produce clay *bodies*, having good working and firing properties. In its plastic or workable state, clay contains between 20 per cent and 30 per cent of water. Most of this is 'free' water and approximately 6 per cent is chemically combined water. A good clay will have plasticity. It will be neither sticky nor *short* (crumbly) and will retain change in shape. This plasticity is explained by comparing the very minute, flat clay particles to sheets of wet glass which will slither and slide yet remain stuck together in spite of all the movement. Clay can be rolled, squeezed and pinched without splitting and cracking and will be fairly strong and easily handled when dry or *green*. Very often, *grog*, which is ground-down, fired clay, is added to the body. This reduces shrinkage and warping. Also fluxes and refractory materials may be added to give the body desirable firing properties. Depending on the body there will be noticeable shrinkage varying between 8 per cent and 15 per cent.

CLASSIFICATIONS

For the potter, there are three general classifications of clay bodies which relate to the firing temperature of the finished piece.

Earthenware	– Red, buff or white	980–1100°C
Stoneware	– Grey, buff or white: vitreous, non-porous	1200–1300°C
Porcelain	– White: vitreous, non-porous, translucent if thin	1250–1400°C

PREPARATION

Dry clay can be reconstituted by adding an excess of water and allowing it to soak for a few days. When the clay has softened and settled it is said to have *slaked*. (Leather-hard clay will not slake very readily and, therefore, should be left to dry completely to a state where it will quickly soak up water.) The excess water is scooped off and the resulting slip or slurry is then dried on a plaster bat until it is plastic. It then has to be thoroughly mixed to a homogeneous consistency. This mixing can be carried out in a *pug mill*, which is rather like a meat mincer in that the clay is forced through a cylinder by a revolving screw. Even if the clay has been pugged, it will still require further preparation before it is ready for use. Unless the pug mill is of a special de-airing type, it is necessary to *wedge* and/or *knead* the clay on a bench to rid it of any tiny pockets of air.

In *wedging* (figure 1.1), a mass of clay which can be easily lifted is sliced with a wire into two halves. One half is lifted, turned through 90° and brought sharply down on the other to promote mixing and to expel air. The mass is lifted, turned through 90° and the process is repeated, systematically slicing and slamming until the clay looks and feels thoroughly mixed. To avoid trapping air when one wedge is slapped down on the other, the wedge on the table can be patted to a slightly convex shape first and any bits such as dry clay, plaster, etc., can be removed. By running a finger along the cut surface, you can test for any variation in consistency (figure 1.2).

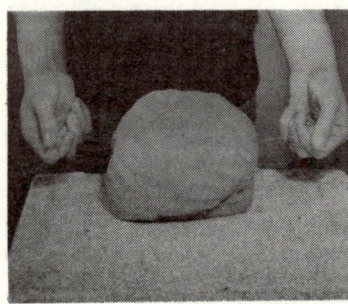

Figure 1.1 Wedging – Slicing the clay

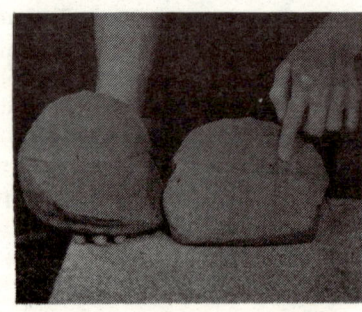

Figure 1.2 Wedging – Testing for any variation in consistency

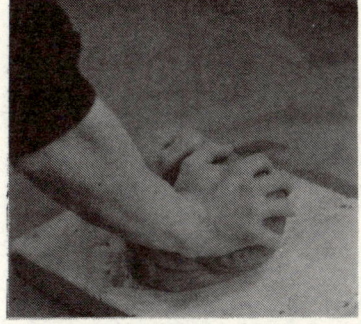

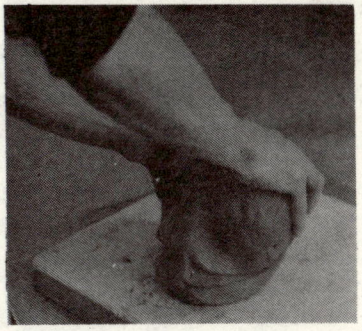

Figure 1.3   Kneading – Folding the clay to mix it and to expel any pockets of air

Figure 1.4   Lifting the mass of clay from the back – note the 'ram's head' appearance

Kneading (figure 1.3) is a rhythmic, folding method of mixing clay. Clay can be kneaded just prior to wheel work to align the clay particles in the direction of the rotation of the wheel, but this is not strictly necessary. The easiest method of kneading is to take a piece of clay of up to about 4.5 kg (10 lb) in weight. Form the clay into a rough block and, lifting rhythmically from the back with your fingers, fold and press down with the palms of your hands, using the whole weight of your body, transferred through your straight arms, to turn the clay over on itself (figure 1.4). A shape similar to a ram's head will result, and any tendency for the shape to become too elongated should be checked by an inward pull with both hands as the clay is lifted from the back.

If a coarse-textured clay is required, it is possible to add up to 20 per cent of grog or sand during the wedging process. This is best done when the clay is fairly wet and it is necessary to ensure an even distribution throughout. Grogged clay is desirable for large slab-built structures since it helps in reducing warping and shrinkage.

2

Tools

In claywork the hands and fingers may be considered to be the most important tools, but a simple personal tool kit is also necessary. A basic tool kit (figure 2.1) can be put together with little expense and, although most tools in general use can be purchased from good craft shops and suppliers of ceramic materials, it is quite easy to improvise certain items.

Special tools such as *turning tools* and *hole-cutters*, and larger items such as *rolling pins* will often be available in the pottery studio, but it is better and more convenient to provide yourself with small items which you will become accustomed to using.

A *cutting wire* is very important for preparing, trimming and releasing clay. It may be made of steel or brass, preferably of the twisted type to avoid kinking, or nylon, and should have toggles (for example, buttons) fitted at either end. Small knives are necessary for trimming and fettling. A potter's knife need not necessarily be sharp, but a pointed shape is desirable to avoid stretching and tearing the clay. A small kitchen knife may be cut down to the right shape. Flexible *kidneys* of steel, for scraping and surface work, may have to be bought but a plastic substitute, cut to shape, may be used. Modelling tools can be purchased in a variety of shapes. They are usually made from hard wood or plastic and, depending on their type, are used for detail shaping, trimming and texturing clay. Metal tools of mild or

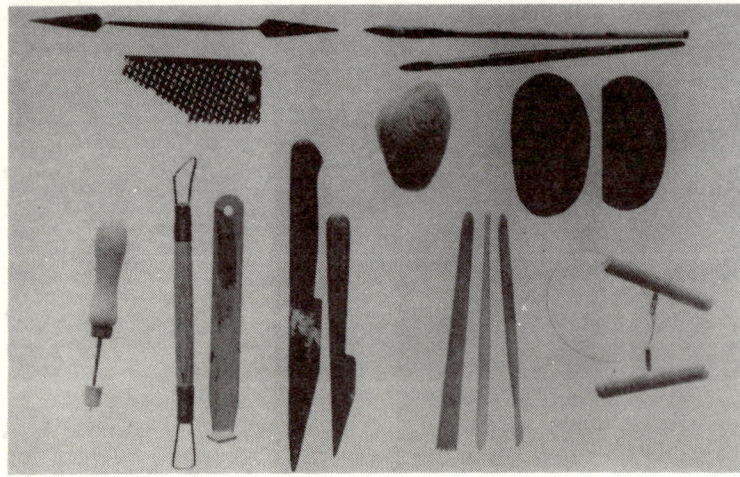

Figure 2.1   A selection of basic tools (left to right) Top – Cutting Wire, Modelling Tools, Knives, Turning Tools and Looped Wire Tool, Clay Needle: Centre – Steel and Rubber Kidneys, Natural Sponge: Bottom – Brushes, 'Keying' Tools

4

stainless steel are available and are especially useful on hard clay. Modelling tools can be improvised from lollipop sticks, miscellaneous kitchen utensils, etc., by re-shaping and cutting down.

Other useful objects include combs and broken hacksaw blades for use as *keying* tools; pen tops, buttons, etc., for impressed decoration; blunt darning needles (kept in a cork for safety) for pricking and scratching clay, and old surform blades for shaping hard clay or plaster. It is a good idea to have one or two artist's-type brushes for applying slip and for decorating.

For wheel work a small, natural sponge or a piece of chamois leather may be required. Turning tools and looped wire tools may have to be borrowed or bought, but again it is possible to make or improvise when you are aware of what is needed.

A protective garment such as an old shirt or apron is a necessity.

Modelling

Figure 3.1   Initial clay experience in squeezing, pinching and extending;
rolling, carving, building and joining

Figure 3.2   Modelling – Small objects, can be made using pinching, rolling,
carving and joining methods. Slip is used when joining clay and modelling
tools may be necessary for detail work

The various characteristics of clay will soon become apparent when you handle it for the first time. You will feel a natural urge to squeeze, pinch and push, and this initial manipulation and exploration (figure 3.1) will soon lead you to discover that clay will not only take on almost any change in form but that it will also retain that change. It is also more responsive and malleable than many synthetic modelling materials, and has a more pleasing feel.

In its plastic state clay can be pinched and rolled out and extended to make thin delicate forms. Pieces can readily be joined one to another. In a drier state, known as *leather hard*, when its consistency resembles Cheddar cheese, it can be carved and 'subtracted'. It can still be joined at this stage, but it is necessary to scratch or *key* all surfaces to be joined with a suitable tool and bond with slip. When dry or green it can be carved, scraped and sanded, though this last will produce unhygienic dust. Although extremely versatile, clay does have certain limitations and there are a few points you need to be aware of.

In its plastic state clay contains about 20 per cent water, and a certain amount of drying out will take place as it is handled. If slight cracks appear on the surface these need to be smoothed over with the finger, at right angles to the crack. Avoid excessive dampening of the form since this will only render the surface slimy and will do little to make good any cracks. A good, well prepared clay should not dry out too quickly unless excessively handled, and a damp (not wet) sponge or cloth will help to keep it workable.

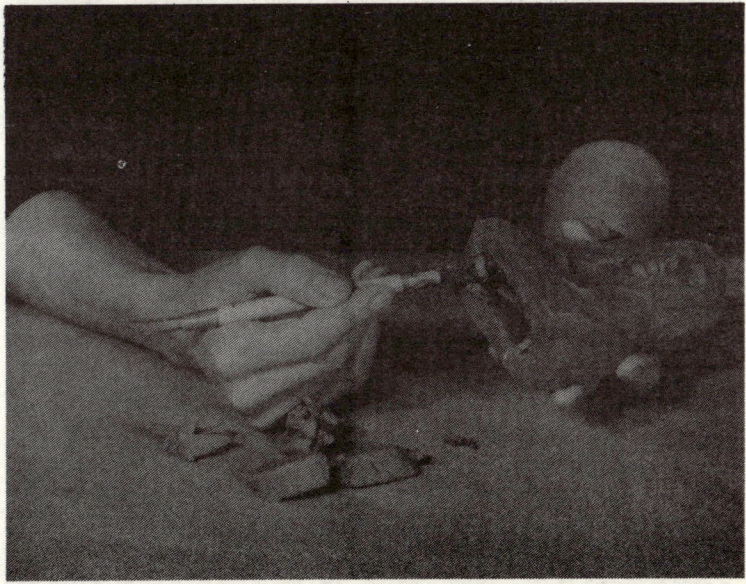

Figure 3.3   Hollowing out a solid form prior to detail finishing, using a looped wire tool to extract the clay

Very thin delicate forms may need support while drying out and this is best done with small props made of the same clay, which will dry and shrink at the same rate as the form. Such delicate forms, particularly those with extensions, are liable to breakage, especially in the dry state prior to biscuit firing and should be treated carefully.

Solid forms will not fire if they are too thick, because the water in the clay turns to steam during firing and, in escaping, may cause the form to shatter. Therefore solid models need to be hollowed out with a looped wire tool (figure 3.3) to achieve, if possible, a wall of regular thickness which will allow the form to dry at an even rate. [A maximum thickness of approximately 12–25 mm (½–1 in.) depending on the grog content of the clay.] This hollowing out will make the piece suitable for firing and will also save weight and clay.

Detail modelling may require the use of modelling tools and these can be improvised to suit as particular needs arise.

Figure 3.4   'Village' Bowl, stoneware – Ian Godfrey (by courtesy of the Hampshire Museum Service)

4

Pinching

Figure 4.1   Pinching between thumb and fingers with the palm of the other
hand supporting the form

This is the technique of making hollow shapes in the hand. Start by
making a ball of soft plastic clay which fits comfortably in the palm
of your hand. Right-handed people usually find it easier to support
the clay in the left hand, while left-handed people will probably need
to change these directions round. An initial opening is made in the
ball with the right thumb, and this is followed by a rhythmic turning
and pinching between thumb on the inside and fingers on the outside (figure 4.1). The left hand turns the clay in an anti-clockwise
direction and the cupped palm produces a rounded bowl shape. An
even thickness throughout is desirable and it is best to concentrate on
the lower half of the bowl at first, otherwise if a thin rim is made too
quickly it may dry out and split. Light tapping of the rim will help in
achieving a regular shape.

It is possible to make very thin pinch pots if the clay is fine and of
good plasticity. By over-pinching one can make a feature of splits and
irregularities, producing forms perhaps resembling fungi, leaves or
petals. Heavily grogged clays, however, do not lend themselves so well
to delicate forms and are usually best suited, unashamedly, to stur-
dier, heavier pieces.

Figure 4.2   Adding a foot. Note that the bowl has been keyed to help the join

Figure 4.3   Smoothing in the foot, with some variations in shape

Bowl shapes can often accommodate the addition of a simple foot (figures 4.2 and 4.3). This can be made from a thin coil or a small, flattened ball, thumbed on to the base. Keying and the addition of slip may be necessary if the pot has dried a little. Care with proportion can result in a pinch pot that has both simplicity and a refined elegance.

Two pinch pots of identical size and about 6 mm (¼ in.) in thickness can be joined together to make hollow spheres or 'eggs'. Both rims should be keyed and slipped, and, as the two pots are offered up to each other, a slight twisting movement will help joining (figures 4.4 and 4.5). Resistance to this twisting pressure is a good sign that the two halves are bonding together. Clay is drawn across the seam with a finger while the form is supported in the palm of the other hand. Air trapped inside will help prevent distortion.

These hollow eggs can serve as a basis for many things and at this point, I would suggest you use your imagination! The egg can be

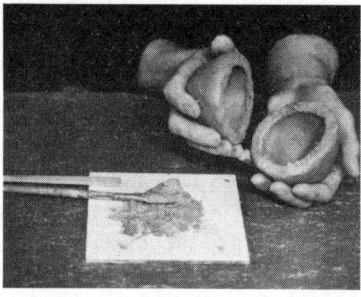

Figure 4.4   Joining two pinch pots; the edges have been keyed and coated with slip

Figure 4.5   Bonding the two pinch pots together by smoothing across the seam. The three forms shown here are derived from the shapes of pebbles and a sea-shell

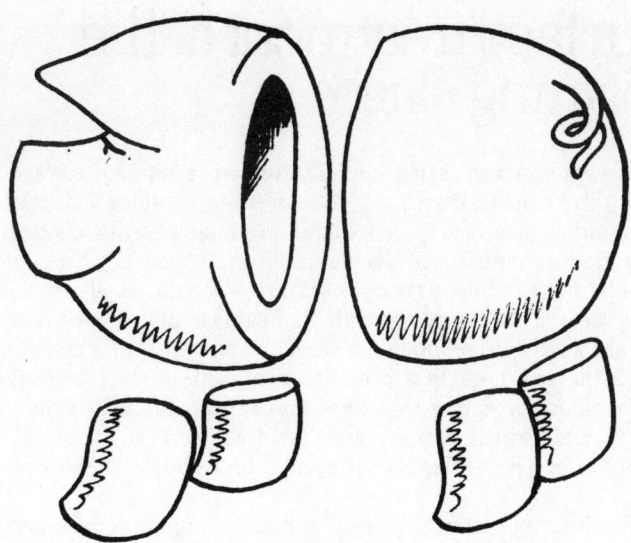

Figure 4.6 How to make a piggy bank from two pinch pots. The face is pinched and modelled and the legs, tail and ears are added. The slot is made with a thin blade or a clay needle

modified to suit your ideas: you can tap it to alter the shape, you can carve into it to produce windows, you can add to it, you can pinch it or change the surface texture. If the completed object has no holes or perforations as part of its design, a small hole should be made in a suitable place underneath. This will assist in drying. It will not necessarily prevent explosion in the kiln; this is usually the result of dampness when the object is fired before it is thoroughly dried out, or when there is too rapid a climb in temperature, so that the small amount of moisture still in the clay turns quickly to steam and shatters the form when escaping through the clay wall.

5

Surface treatment at the forming stages

Clay work can very often benefit from some kind of surface treatment: clay's intrinsic response to impressing, combing and scratching, for example, can readily be exploited to emphasise its 'clayness' and to add. both visual and tactile interest. In general, decoration — whether it be in line, pattern or texture — should usually enhance the form and be in sympathy with it. For example, a bowl will more happily accept decoration of a curved nature than of a straight, geometric nature; lines that echo its own shape or that emphasise its round character, rather than lines that seem to sit awkwardly on the surface and distract. Simple, restrained treatment can effectively bring emphasis to a particular part of a piece, for example, the shoulder of a pot.

Texture and pattern can also be used to disguise some irregularity. You should be careful not to over-decorate; areas of roughened surface are often complemented by smoother areas. Of course there are exceptions to the rule; sometimes the clay form can serve as a 'canvas' or ground for imagery that has a more primary purpose than simply enhancing the form.

IMPRESSING
Anything which is harder than the plastic clay can be used to alter the surface. Rhythmic repetition with the simplest of tools (even a finger

Figure 5.1   Impressed decoration using folded card and sundry 'found' objects

Figure 5.2   Carved and incised decoration on two slab pots. The large, square pot features circles within squares, and the effect is emphasised with iron oxide in the recesses. The small pot has oval lines, to echo its oval shape, scratched in when the clay was dry

nail) will produce impressed pattern and texture. 'Found objects' such as folded card, pen tops and modelling tools are ideal (figure 5.1). Stippled textured areas can be made with the bristles of a toothbrush or the repeated application of a pointed instrument. Special stamps or seals can be made by carving your initials or mark, in reverse, in a small piece of leather-hard clay, which is then biscuit fired.

Linear decoration or drawn images can be impressed by repeating with a suitable thin, flat tool and this is neater than scratching, since no burred edges are raised. The clay itself can be rolled or pressed against hessian, tree bark, floors, etc., to pick up surface interest.

COMBING, INCISING AND SCRATCHING
Hatched lines and linear patterns can be drawn on the surface of the clay, preferably at the leather-hard stage, with pointed tools and toothed objects such as combs and hacksaw blades. Roughened areas, which contrast effectively with smooth areas, both to sight and feel, can be made by combing in various directions. Lines scratched into dry clay will have a sharper, less fluid quality (figure 5.2).

CARVING AND PIERCING
Deeper cuts and grooves can be made by extracting strips of clay with a looped wire tool or with paper clips. At the leather-hard stage it is possible to pierce through the clay to make 'windows' or to effect a lattice appearance (figures 5.3 and 5.4). This is best done with a thin-bladed knife or a scalpel. It is also possible to pierce the clay with a drill when it is dry or at the biscuit stage.

Figure 5.3   Carved and pierced bowl (leather hard) — Alvin Betteridge

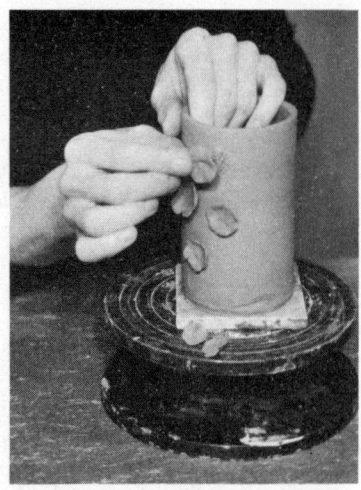

Figure 5.4   Puzzle Jug, thrown and pierced, stoneware with iron and cobalt oxides — Martin Brothers, late 19th century (courtesy of Mrs. I. Withers)

Figure 5.5   Applied decoration using roughened and slipped surfaces

APPLYING AND MODELLING

Clay can be added and built up in the form of strips, thin coils, pellets and pre-formed shapes for relief effect (figure 5.5). When adding clay, ensure that both surface and the added clay are of the same consistency, otherwise they may dry and shrink at different rates and lose adhesion. Slip is necessary to join applied decoration at the leather-hard stage.

SPRIGGING

This is a form of applied decoration where a small relief image in soft clay is pre-formed in a plaster or biscuit mould and then added to the surface of a form (figure 5.6). An original model for a sprig motif can be made in clay and then a mould is made in plaster as described in the section on one-piece mould making in chapter 8. An existing object such as a fancy button, could be used as a model as long as care is taken to ensure there is no gap underneath which will allow the plaster to run under the model, so trapping it. A gap can be avoided by lightly pressing the model into a bed of clay before making the mould.

A design can be carved into a piece of clay which is then fired, to produce a mould. Alternatively, hard plaster could be used. From this hollow pattern (*intaglio*) a relief image (*cameo*) is produced when soft clay is pressed in.

Thin, delicate sprigs should obviously be handled carefully. After excess clay is scraped from the mould, the sprig can usually be imme-

Figure 5.6   Sprigging – pre-formed relief decoration using simple biscuit and plaster moulds

diately tapped out gently and applied to the desired place with a coating of slip. As with all clay joining, this can be done up to and including the leather-hard stage.

EXTRUDING
Soft clay can be forced through a perforated vessel such as a colander or a tea strainer (figure 5.7). This will produce tiny clay 'worms' which can be used effectively for textured surfaces such as a 'woolly coat' on a model of a sheep, or coarse grass on a ceramic landscape.

Great care must be exercised throughout. The surface to which the tiny extrusions are to be applied should first be coated with slip, and then the clay should be extruded on to something like a thin palette knife which is then used to transfer the worms to the slipped surface. Such delicate work will need careful handling even after the piece is glaze fired.

Figure 5.7   Extruding clay through a tea strainer to make 'grass' and 'foliage' for a ceramic landscape

15

6

Coiling

Coiling is the technique of building with long rolls of clay which are bonded together as the form grows. It is a very versatile method and can be used to make large forms of a pre-determined shape. Also, because it is of a 'contemplative' and 'growing' nature, pieces can be intuitive and improvised.

Like other hand-forming methods, there is great potential in coil building and, because it has its own characteristics, it should never be thought of as in any way inferior to wheel work.

The clay required should be quite soft and of a plastic consistency. Clay that is stiff will not lend itself to the handling which the method involves without drying and splitting. A fairly substantial pot of 250–300 mm (10–12 in.) in height can be attempted at the outset by anyone first using the method.

There are numerous ways of making a base. A wide, thick pinch pot may be used if a rounded foundation is desired. Alternatively, a circle can be cut from a slab of clay 12–19 mm (½–¾ in.) thick, using a suitable object as a template. This is more suitable for large pieces because an even thickness is more easily achieved. Another method is to make a ball of clay about 10 g (6 oz) in weight, or the size of a tomato, and to pat this down to form a round disc of little finger thickness (figure 6.1). The base is then placed on a piece of paper or a wooden or plaster bat to prevent it from sticking to the work surface. (If you are attending a pottery course it may be wise to mark the base with your initials underneath now, because it may be more difficult later on.)

Rolling coils requires a little practice, so don't worry if they are not quite right at the first attempt. A wooden board or table is necessary, because its absorbent surface will stop the clay from sticking. Take a piece of clay in your hand and make a sausage shape. Then, using the full length and width of the palm of the hand, roll the sausage along the work surface, applying gentle and even pressure as you roll (figure 6.2). Try to ensure that it rolls through a complete

Figure 6.1   Making a base for a coil pot from a ball of clay

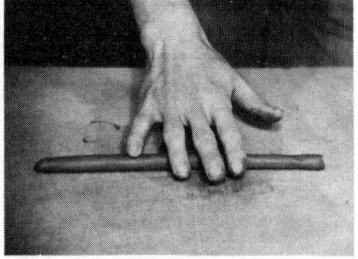

Figure 6.2   Rolling a coil

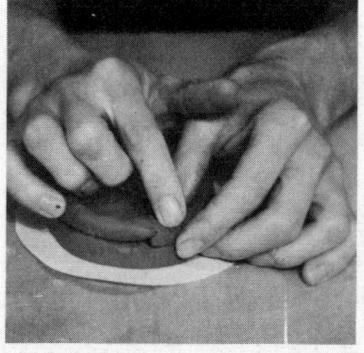
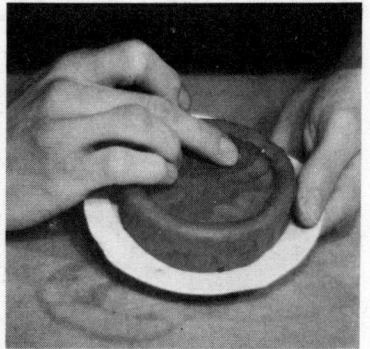

Figure 6.3   Joining the two ends of   Figure 6.4   Bonding the first coil
              the coil

revolution by moving from the base of the palm to the finger-tips, and this should keep it round in section. If at first it does make an oval shape, then gently tap it back to a round section and try again.

By moving your hand along the length of the clay as you roll, it is possible to make a long, even coil of about the same thickness as the little finger. If this seems to be rather thick, you'll understand why when you start building because a little clay thickness is lost in the bonding process. It is desirable to make a coil long enough to go around the top of the base so that there is only one join. You can, if you wish, roll enough lengths to make a number of coils, as long as they are kept under a damp cloth until required.

Although fairly soft clay is used in this method, it is still a good habit to key lightly the clay surfaces to be joined, so the perimeter of the top of the base can be scratched with a suitable tool.

The first coil is now placed around the top of the base and the excess length is pinched off. The two ends are joined together by gently pushing a little clay from one to the other (figure 6.3), at right angles to the join. Then the coil itself is bonded to the base with an up-and-down movement with the tip of the finger (figure 6.4), inside and out, so that base and coil become as one. The next coil is made (or taken from under the damp cloth, if previously rolled) and placed on the first one. This can be bonded to the previous coil at this stage, or it is possible to build a few coils and bond them at the same time. It is wise not to have the joined ends of the coils in the same place above each other, because this may cause a weakness in the structure.

At this stage the work can be transferred to a banding wheel (figure 6.5) to help achieve regularity and symmetry (if desired). The piece can be made fuller by slightly lengthening each coil and placing it on the outer edge of the one underneath. Conversely, it can be made narrower by slightly shortening each coil and placing it on the inner edge. I say 'slightly' because any sudden change of direction may

Figure 6.5   Thumbing-in a coil. Note how the other hand supports the wall of
the pot

cause the pot to sag. Gentle curves are easier to cope with initially.
Very often it is necessary to allow some drying to take place before
adding more height and subsequent weight. This is especially so with
rotund shapes. If you are attending a weekly course, a large pot may
take a number of weeks to build and needs to be kept wrapped in
plastic sheeting. Slight drying will probably take place between
sessions and it will certainly be necessary to key the surface of the top
coil before adding more.

When the pot is complete it can be smoothed down with the finger,
or a damp sponge, and then perhaps decorated with an impressed
pattern. At the leather-hard stage it can be beaten or *paddled* with a
flat stick, or worked on with a scraper (figures 6.6 and 6.7) to make
the final shape and surface.

The coils themselves can be used as a decorative surface feature.
They can, if even enough, be left exposed on the outside or 'thumbed'
at regular intervals to provide partial joining and visual and tactile
interest (figure 6.8). If this is desired, then it is essential to be thorough with all inside joins as the piece grows. Also I think it is often
necessary to join the bottom couple of coils and, say, the top two
coils on the outside, to give the pot a foundation and a 'conclusion'.

Coils can also be effectively exploited by building inside a plaster
mould (figure 6.9). A plastic bowl may be used but this will need to

Figure 6.6   Beating or 'paddling' the coil pot to achieve the desired shape. The lower part is wrapped in polythene because it is drier than the rest of the pot. This helps the whole piece to dry slowly and uniformly

Figure 6.7   Scraping the leather hard pot with a flexible steel kidney to refine the surface

19

Figure 6.8   Coiled forms

Figure 6.9   Coiling inside a plaster mould, exploiting the patterns of the coils. Hanging bowls can be made this way and different coiled patterns can be tried

20

Figure 6.10   Making a bowl on a plaster hump mould. Here the coil pattern is seen on the inside. A coiled foot ring has been added to the finished bowl. Thorough bonding of the coils is essential when one side is left as a decorative feature in this way

Figure 6.11   Coiled form, carved and pierced with glaze brushed on in selected areas, stoneware – Anne Bradley

be lined with paper to prevent the clay from sticking. This is suitable for making hanging bowls because the coil shapes can be seen from underneath. The opposite effect can be achieved by building on the outside of a hump-mould (figure 6.10). The coil pattern will then be seen on the inside.

As I mentioned earlier, coiling can be used as a means to an end in making preconceived forms of either a symmetrical or an assymmetrical nature, with coils made to suitable thickness for larger pieces, or it can be intuitive. By this, I mean you can just start building and see how it develops. The method can suggest its own direction and some very interesting ceramics, using the rhythm and dynamics of the coils, can result.

7

Slabbing

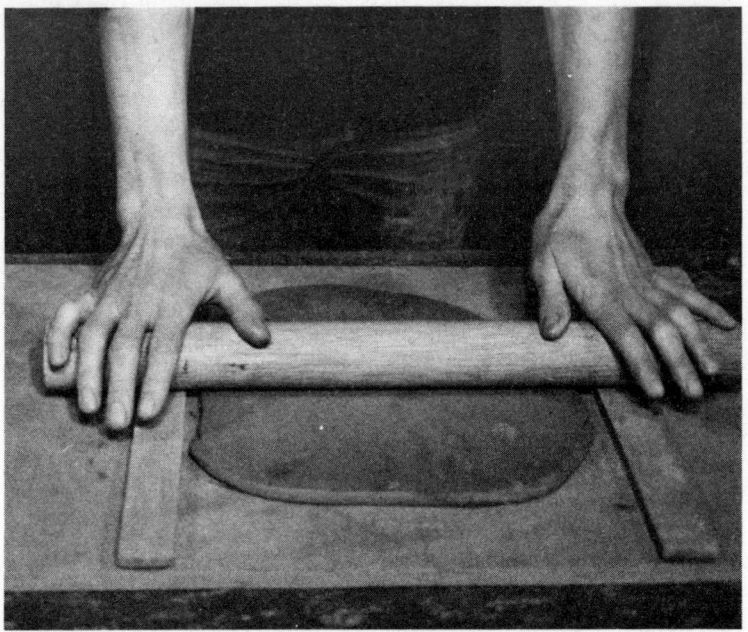

Figure 7.1   Rolling out a sheet of clay with wooden guides at either side to
ensure an even thickness

'This is a kind of ceramic joinery and provided the designs derive from
the nature of the material it offers yet another wide range of ex-
pression.' So states Bernard Leach in *A Potter's Book.*

The slab form is usually preconceived, with component parts made
from flat sheets of clay, cut to size and assembled. Clay is rolled out
on a flat surface with a rolling pin (figure 7.1). To achieve an even
thickness, which is usually desirable to prevent uneven drying and distortion, two sticks of equal thickness, known as guides, are placed
either side of the clay. The surface on which the slab is made should
be of porous material such as wood, otherwise the clay will stick. A
rolling-out surface of some kind of textile such as hessian will enable
the slab to be moved without undue handling and stretching, and this
can also be used to impart texture to the clay surface. Start by rolling
from the centre of the mass of clay, working from a standing position
so that the weight of your body can be effectively transferred through
your arms. If a textile surface is not used it will probably be necessary
to move the clay around the board frequently to prevent it from sticking. When the rolling pin ceases to make any impression on the clay
then you will have a slab of even thickness, the same as the guides.

As an alternative to rolling, sheets can be made by drawing a wire harp through a large mass of clay. A harp is a special U-shaped tool, with notches at regular intervals on both arms to which the cutting wire is attached. By moving the wire up or down the notches, a number of regular slabs can be quickly made when the harp is drawn horizontally through the clay.

When the slabs have been made, pieces of the desired shape may be cut using the rolling guides (figure 7.2) to obtain straight edges. Templates can be made from paper or card.

It is usually necessary with all but very small forms to leave slabs to dry to a leather-hard state before cutting and assembling the pieces. This is certainly the case with precise forms of a rectangular nature. It is essential that all joins be thoroughly keyed and slipped before assembly. You can either brush slip on to the keyed surface or, after cross-hatching you can brush on water and then key again, so breaking down some clay particles and actually making slip from the slabs to be joined. As was described in the joining of two pinch pots, resistance to a sliding movement is a sign of a good join.

Sides should be added on top of a base, not to the edge of it, so that both sides of the seam can be bonded. Tall forms should be built lying down, with one side initially serving as a base. Coils of clay should be used for extra strengthening on all inside angles and should be neatly modelled in (figure 7.5). To prevent warping, large slabbed forms should be allowed to dry slowly. Partial covering in polythene will help this.

A small pot can be made from a rectangular slab measuring approximately 200 x 100 mm (8 x 4 in.) — figures 7.3a to d. The two short edges are keyed and slipped then joined to make a cylindrical or perhaps an oval, 'rounded square' or triangular tube. This is then stood

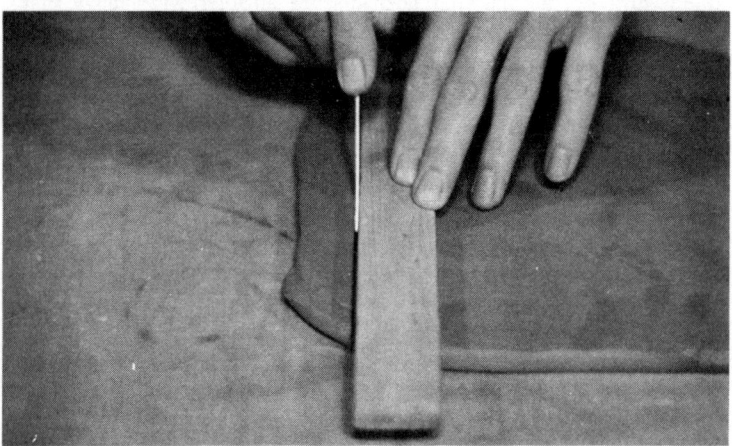

Figure 7.2   Cutting slabs, using a rolling guide for a straight edge. Note that the knife is kept vertical so that the cut edges remain square

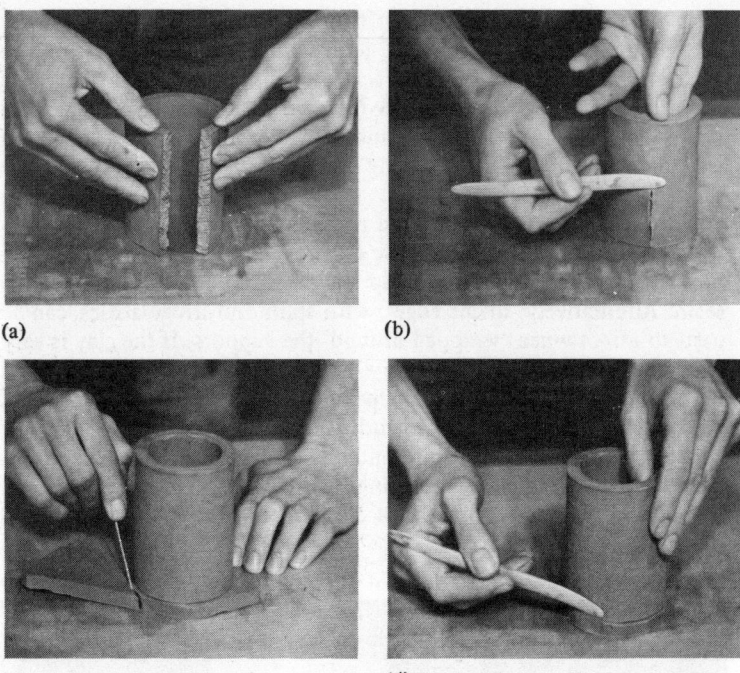

(a)   (b)

(c)   (d)

Figure 7.3   (a) Making a simple slabbed cylinder — joining the keyed edges
              (b) Smoothing the seam (not forgetting the inside)
              (c) Cutting a base
              (d) Joining the base

Figure 7.4   Joining sections of a larger
              slabbed form, having keyed and
              slipped the edges

Figure 7.5   Reinforcing the inside
              angle with a coil. If the slabs are
              leather hard it will be necessary
              to roughen the inside angle and
              perhaps use slip so that the coil
              can be effectively bonded

on another slab and a base is cut to fit. The edge of the tube and the base are then keyed, slipped and joined and all the seams are smoothed over by drawing a little clay across the seam with your finger or a modelling tool (figures 7.3d and 7.4). A simple mug can be made in this way with a strip of clay cut and shaped to make a handle. The top edge can be refined by smoothing away the sharp edges with a damp sponge.

Soft slabs can be built around paper-covered supports such as rolling pins or sections of drain pipe (figure 7.6). The two edges can be brought together, joined with slip and then smoothed off to lose the seam. Alternatively, uncut edges, with splits and irregularities, can be used to effect when 'wrapped around' the support. If the clay is very soft, keying may not be necessary, but small objects can be impressed on the overlapping sections to help the joining and to decorate.

The whole piece, support included, can now be stood on a slab of clay and a base can be cut to fit and modelled in place. When the form has dried a little, the paper covering the support will allow the support to be removed and small coils of clay can be placed, if necessary, in the inside seam of the base.

Figure 7.6   Using a paper covered support to build with soft slabs. Here any splits and irregularities are retained as a feature and impressed decoration is used on the over-lapping sections

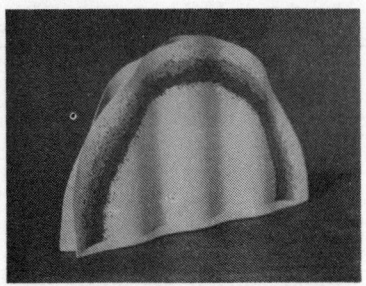

Figure 7.7   Refining the surface of a
slabbed dish when leather hard,
using a steel kidney

Figure 7.8   Triple Ripple Vase, porcelain – Tony Franks (courtesy
of Portsmouth Museum and Art
Gallery)

Because of the precise nature of many slab-built forms, a certain
amount of finishing can be carried out at the leather-hard stage or
when the form is dry. Flat-sided forms can be scraped with a wood or
steel straight-edged tool (figure 7.7). This fettling should, however, be
carefully carried out, because dry clay is very fragile. When carving
and scraping, try to support the area which is being worked on, and
don't try to remove too much clay at a time.

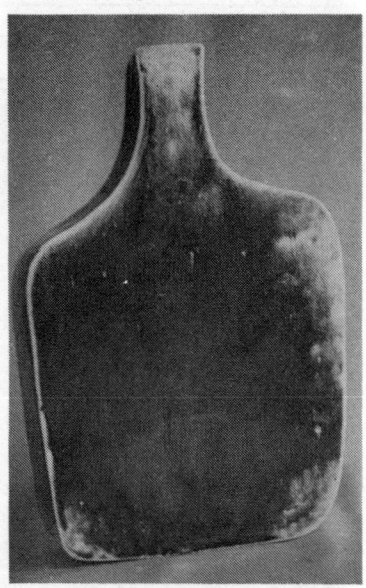

Figure 7.9   Caesar's Wardrobe, slab
built and modelled, earthenware
– David Hamilton (courtesy of
Southampton Art Gallery)

Figure 7.10 Asymmetric bottle, earthenware – Sybil Bunn

8

Mould making, pressing and casting

MOULD MAKING

A *mould* is a foundation from which impressions (casts) can be taken. Because clay so readily takes impressions, moulds can play an important part in studio ceramics, especially when it is desired to reproduce forms. Moulds are usually made of plaster of Paris, which is very absorbent and will allow clay cast on it, or in it, to dry and shrink without sticking. Moulds can also be made from clay which is then biscuit fired. A biscuit mould can simply be a fired clay dish or a low hump, formed either by hand or centred on a wheel.

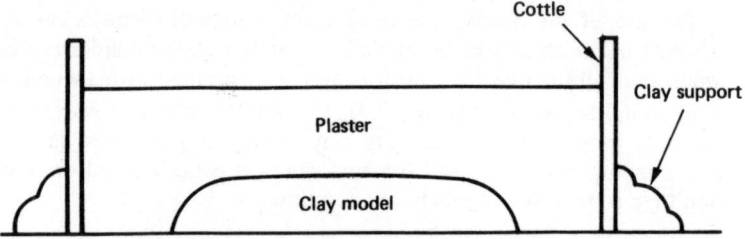

Figure 8.1   Making a plaster concave mould – sectioned diagram

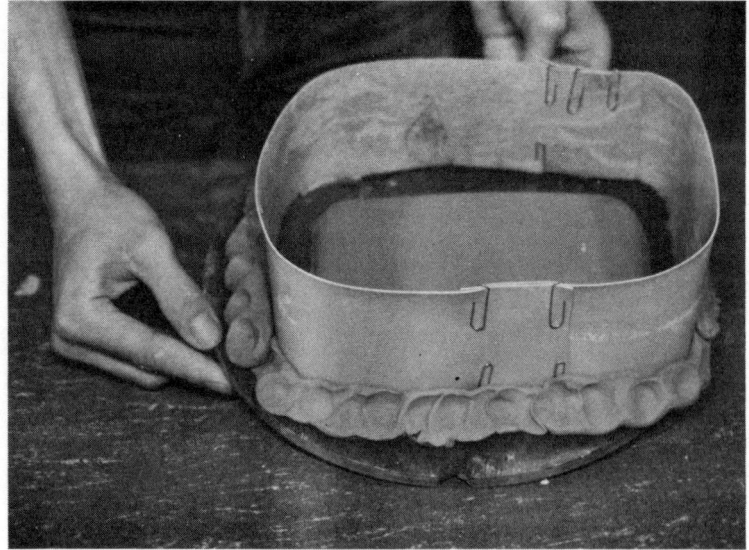

Figure 8.2   Making a plaster concave mould – the solid clay model is surrounded by a cottle made of lino to retain the plaster. Any gaps in the cottle are filled with clay

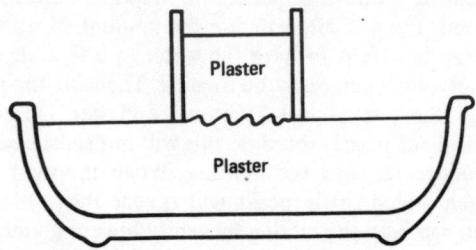

Figure 8.3   Making a plaster mushroom mould – sectioned diagram. Here an existing dish is used to make the main part of the mould and then a cottle is made, from lino or perhaps a plastic container with its base removed, to retain the plaster for the stem of the mould

MAKING A PLASTER ONE-PIECE MOULD

A *one-piece mould* is the simplest type and can be a convex, hump shape (male) or a concave, dish shape (female). A concave plaster mould is made around some kind of suitable shape or former (figures 8.1 and 8.2). This original shape, known as a model, will determine the shape of the mould and subsequent casts taken from the mould. A plaster hump mould can be made from the inside of an existing dish (figure 8.3). This could be of glass, ceramic or plastic. Some kind of release agent, such as soft soap, will need to be coated inside the dish first so that the plaster, when dry, can be extracted. A stem can be made for this type of mould by placing a cardboard tube (or a plastic cup with its base cut off) on the first part of the mould, just before it sets hard. This is then filled with more plaster. If the first part has set hard, it will be necessary to roughen up the surface before making the stem, so that the two will bond together. This mould is sometimes called a 'mushroom mould' because of its shape.

A concave mould can be made over a suitable existing object or over a specially made clay model. This clay model can be hump-shaped on a wheel, or if a shape other than round is required then the model is formed from a mass of clay smoothed down to the right shape, by hand or with the aid of a template. There should be no undercuts which will allow the plaster to run under the model and trap it.

When the model has been made, a wall, called a cottle, is built to retain the plaster. This wall needs to be about 50 mm (2 in.) from the model and should be tall enough to allow plaster to cover the model to a depth of about 50 mm. A cottle can be made from card, lino, flexible metal sheeting, sheets of glass, glazed tiles or from coils or slabs of clay.

PLASTER MIXING

Plaster of Paris, often bought as dental plaster, is made from dehydrated gypsum and it very rapidly absorbs water. It is therefore essential when preparing a mix that plaster be added to water, and not the other way round. First of all, estimate the amount of water required to fill the cottle. It is best to have the water in a flexible plastic or a glazed container which can easily be cleaned. Then sift the plaster into the water until the water will take no more plaster. Do not casually throw in handfuls of plaster, because this will not slake easily and will probably introduce air into the mixture. When the right amount of plaster has been added, little peaks will appear above the surface of the water. You can help the mixing by gently lowering your hand into the container to break up any lumps, but do this slowly, otherwise air may get into the mixture. The plaster can then be poured into the cottle and tapping the work bench will help to bring any air bubbles to the surface. If you have underestimated the amount required to cover the model, you will probably have time to mix some more and pour in before the plaster 'goes off'. If it has gone off, roughen up the top surface of the first mix. If you have over-estimated, do not under any circumstances pour the remainder of the mixture down the sink; it will block it. Either pour it on to newspaper or let it set and then scrape it into a waste bin.

When plaster sets, a chemical reaction takes place. After a few minutes it will be quite warm to the touch and this is a good sign. Old plaster, which may have taken in moisture from the atmosphere, may have already partially gone off and will not set hard. It will feel soapy when it does eventually dry. Fresh plaster will feel warm quite quickly and then, after about an hour, when it has cooled again, the cottle can be removed. Now the original model can be released, or carefully dug out if it is made of clay. (Do not try to remove the model when the plaster is still warm, because it is still in a state of expansion.) Finally any sharp edges on the outside of the mould should be smoothed off with a pierced file.

It is absolutely vital that plaster is not allowed to contaminate pottery clay. It will cause fired work to shatter as it expands in the relatively moist atmosphere outside the kiln, so it is necessary that clay used for mould making is kept apart from other clays in use.

MAKING A PLASTER TWO-PIECE MOULD

Objects which are basically spherical in shape can be made from two-piece moulds. Again the model could be a found object such as an apple, an egg or an onion, or can be specially made in clay. A sphere is moulded in two halves, with the join following a line running round the widest part of the sphere so as not to undercut and trap the model. First build up clay to exactly half-way round the model (figure 8.4a). Then make a cottle as described previously and pour in plaster (figure 8.4b). When this has set and cooled, turn the whole thing

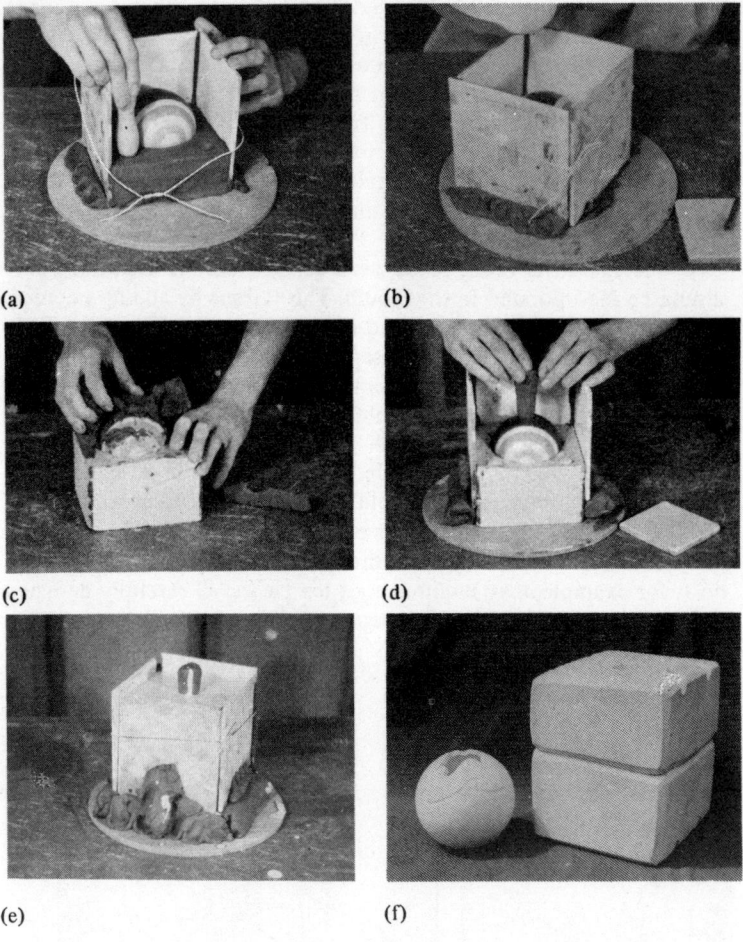

(a)

(b)

(c)

(d)

(e)

(f)

Figure 8.4 (a) Making a two-piece plaster mould. The model, a child's ball, with clay built up to a halfway point. Notches are being made in the clay bed which will locate the two halves of the mould when it is finished. The cottle of glazed tiles is part erected
(b) Pouring in plaster to make the first half of the mould
(c) Removing the clay bed. The model stays in place in the first half of the plaster mould
(d) Building the cottle for the second half of the mould. The face of the first half has been thoroughly soaped so that the second half will not stick. Here a cone of clay is being positioned on the model to form a pouring hole in the mould (for slip casting)
(e) The second half of the mould being made. Note how the cottle is supported with clay and tied with string
(f) The finished two-piece mould – the edges have all been smoothed off with a pierced file

31

over, take away the clay (figure 8.4c) and, if notches were not made in the clay bed, make notches in the face of the first half of the mould. This can be done with a coin or a dinner knife to make hemispherical notches. Then brush on two or three coats of soft soap so that the second half will separate from the first. Check the cottle for any gaps and pour in plaster. After the second half has set and cooled, the two halves will pull apart to release the model and can be later relocated with the notches for casting. To illustrate this procedure I have used a toy ball as a model.

If the mould is going to be used for slip casting a pouring-hole should be incorporated in the mould. This is done by adding a conical shaped piece of clay (narrow end on) to the model (figure 8.4d). If any difficulty is experienced in separating piece moulds from a clay model, soaking in water will cause the model to swell slightly and this will in effect push the plaster mould apart.

All the outside edges of each of the sections of the mould are smoothed off with a pierced file. When the mould is reassembled ready for slip casting, it can be held together with cord or with rubber bands cut from the inner tube of a car tyre.

More complex shapes will require more than two pieces. A detailed bust, for example, may require about ten pieces, all carefully designed to avoid trapping the model (see figures 8.5, 8.6 and 8.7).

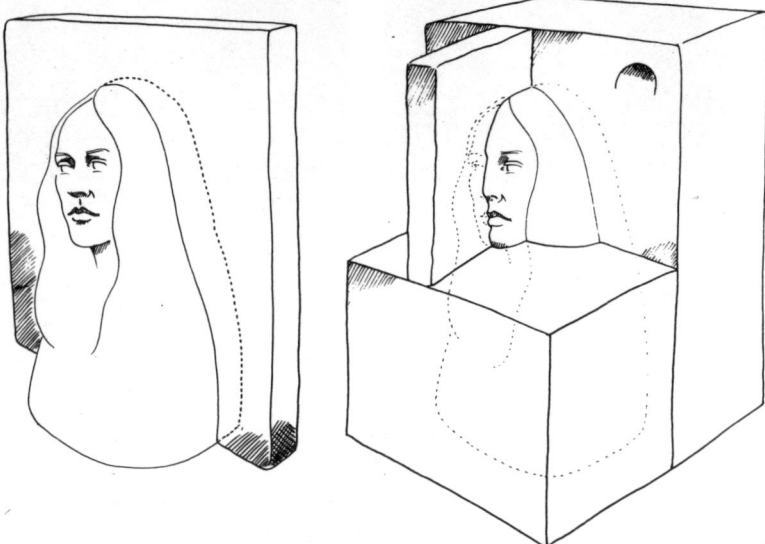

Figure 8.5   Making a piece-mould —
diagram showing how a model
can be divided by using a wall of
clay

Figure 8.6   Making a piece-mould —
diagram showing two pieces of
the mould completed and a clay
wall being used to divide the
upper half of the face

Figure 8.7   A piece-mould in sections with a cast produced from it — the model was first made in clay and then the mould was carefully designed so as not to trap it

PRESSING AND CASTING

Pressing is the technique of forming flat shapes on or in simple moulds. Slabs of clay can be draped over hump moulds to make dish shapes (figure 8.8). Rolling the clay out on hessian will help, so that the clay can be lifted on to the mould more easily. The clay is then smoothed over with a sponge (unless the impressions from the hessian

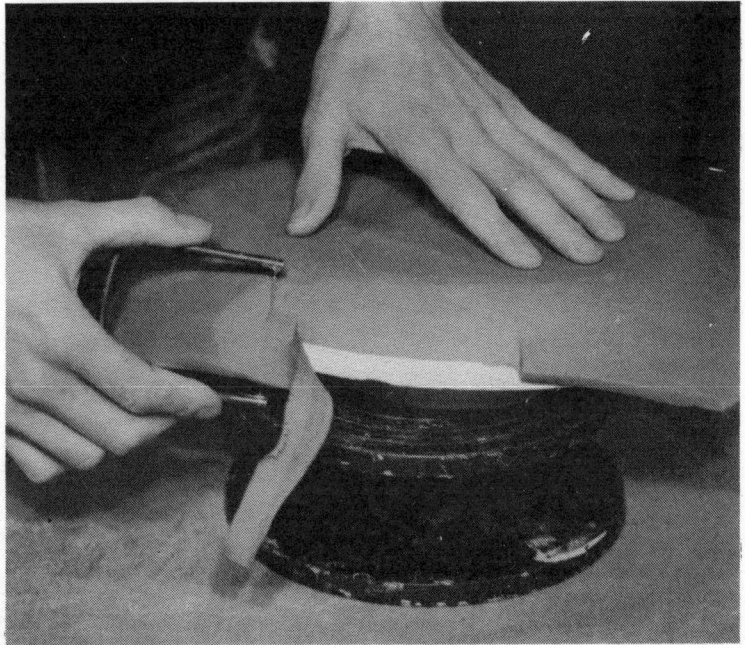

Figure 8.8   Press-moulding on a mushroom mould. Trimming away the excess clay with a small harp

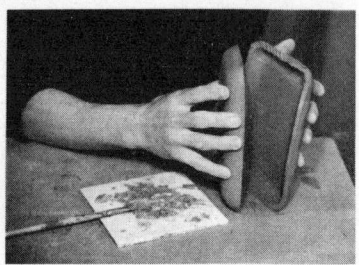

Figure 8.9 Press-moulding a small dish in a concave plaster mould – trimming away the excess clay

Figure 8.10 Joining two press-moulded shapes. The edges of both have been thoroughly keyed and coated with slip

are desired) and the excess clay is trimmed away with a knife or a wire. A coiled or slabbed foot can be added, and the dish is left on the mould to dry. Slip-decorated slabs, when leather hard, can be carefully draped on to hump moulds and then trimmed.

Slabs can also be pressed into concave moulds (figure 8.9), but care should be exercised, otherwise the clay may be stretched and thinned out. Free-standing forms such as flasks and bottles can be made from two pressed dishes. These are carefully joined together (figure 8.10) with slip when leather hard and can be modified as desired by being pierced and modelled (figure 8.11). Two-piece moulds may be used in the same way to make two sections which are then joined together with slip.

Figure 8.11 Two flasks made from two joined, press-moulded shapes, carved and pierced, stoneware glaze

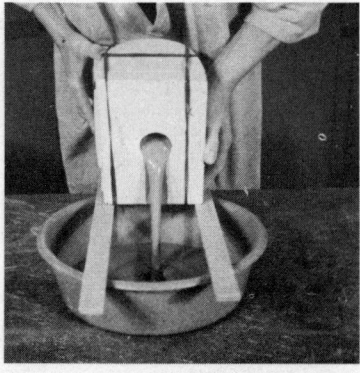 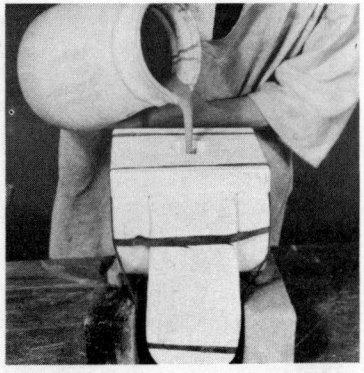

Figure 8.12 Slip casting – filling the mould. This is a multi-piece mould which is bound together with rubber bands made from a motor-car tyre inner tube

Figure 8.13 Slip casting – draining the mould, after which it is left on the sticks to dry off

SLIP CASTING

Piece moulds can be used for *slip casting*. This is a process used widely in industry for reproduction purposes. When slip is poured into a piece mould (figure 8.12), the plaster absorbs water from the slip and after a few minutes, when the excess slip is poured out, a shell of clay is left inside the mould. During casting it is necessary to keep the mould topped up in the pouring-hole as the level sinks down. The thickness of the cast can be checked in the pouring-hole and then the excess slip is slowly poured out and the mould allowed to drain (figure 8.13). Slow pouring is important, because if the slip 'glugs' it may create a vacuum and distort the cast. When the cast is released the seams formed by the joins in the mould are fettled off while the cast is leather hard.

Ordinary slip is unsuitable for casting because of its high water content (about as much water, by weight, as clay). This causes the slip to settle at the bottom of the mould, resulting in uneven casting, undue shrinkage and warping. Also moulds become very wet, considerably slowing up the process, and casts, if they do release freely, are usually brittle. The reason for ordinary slip having a high water content is that normally the minute clay particles gather together in 'flocks'. The particles are attracted electrically and the clay is said to be in a *flocculated* condition, so that a lot of water is needed to make the clay flow. *Casting slip* (which can be bought from most clay suppliers) is made by adding deflocculants, that is, substances which cause the clay particles to repel each other by reversing the minute electrical charge in the clay. A deflocculated slip requires very little water to make the clay flow and is stronger when dry, shrinks less and releases more easily and quickly from the mould. Common deflocculants are sodium

Figure 8.14 Set of three anagrammatical busts: Apollinaire, Epicurus and Juan Gris. Slip-cast porcelain – Ian Hamilton Finlay/Roger Bunn

silicate (water-glass) and soda ash, used together to constitute usually less than half of one per cent of dry weight of clay. It is not possible to give a general recipe because clays used in further education establishments vary tremendously, but some suppliers of clay have casting slip recipes in their catalogues. You can experiment by weighing out some dry clay and then making a smooth paste with water; a drop of sodium silicate and soda ash when added will make a surprising difference to the liquidity of the slip.

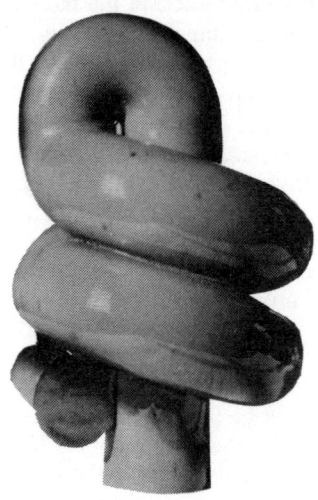

Figure 8.15 Bent Tube Form, earthenware – Delon Cookson (Courtesy of Portsmouth Museum and Art Gallery)

9

Slip

Slip is a solution of clay and water of a semi-fluid consistency, which can be used effectively in a creamy state (engobe) to change the surface and to decorate a form. Slipware has an advantage in that decoration is carried out during the making stages and that usually only a simple transparent earthenware glaze is necessary. The technique is also part of our national heritage and tradition, and many museums have examples of early English slipware pottery.

Metallic oxides or commercially prepared body stains can be used to make different coloured or contrasting slips, if only one basic clay is in general use. Ideally a slip should be made from the same clay as the form to which it is being applied. In this case it will be necessary to break down some dry clay to a powdered state and weigh out a percentage of oxide or stain, adding this to the powdered clay before making the creamy solution with water (see chapter 15). If there are two clays available, say, a red and a buff which are both of a similar consistency, one can be added as a slip over the other. Slip is often produced as a result of wheel work and can be collected and sieved ready for use. Natural shades are usually more suitable for pots; some body stains tend to look too synthetic and unnatural, but may suit models. Slip can be used to decorate work up to and including the leather-hard state and these are the various techniques.

DIPPING OR BRUSHING
When leather hard, a form can be covered wholly or partially with a layer of slip, different in colour or tone from the body. This can be done by dipping, which will usually give a dense, even covering. If there is insufficient quantity for dipping, slip may be brushed on to the surface. Free brush-work decoration is possible if a suitable, soft haired brush is used. For large areas you will need to use a *mop*. This is a full, soft brush which will not leave too many marks. A whirler can be used to effect a covering on round, regular shapes. Ordinary artist's-type bristle brushes can be used if a vigorous, brush-marked effect is sought.

SGRAFFITO
First a piece of work is covered with a layer of slip as described above; then, when almost dry, a suitable pointed tool is used to scratch linear decoration through the layer of slip to reveal the body (figure 9.1).

TRAILING
Lines of a fluid nature can be effected by trailing (figures 9.2 and 9.3). Slip of a creamy consistency is first sieved then put into a slip trailer. This is a flexible rubber or plastic container with a nozzle.

Figure 9.1   Sgraffito − scratching through a layer of red slip to reveal the buff body. The red slip was 'banded' on with a soft brush

Figure 9.2   Slip-trailing

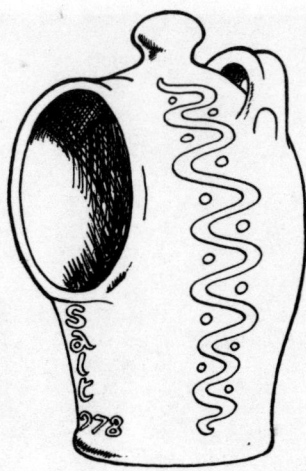

Figure 9.3   Traditional slipware salt kit – usually thrown but could be coil-built

With practice it is possible to draw images and free-flowing lines or create 'trellis' effects.

FEATHERING
First a flat slab of clay is covered with a layer of slip. While this is still wet, parallel lines of contrasting slip are trailed over at regular intervals. Then a feather or a bristle from a broom is drawn carefully at right angles across the trailed lines, resulting in delicate patterns as the slips partially merge (figure 9.4).

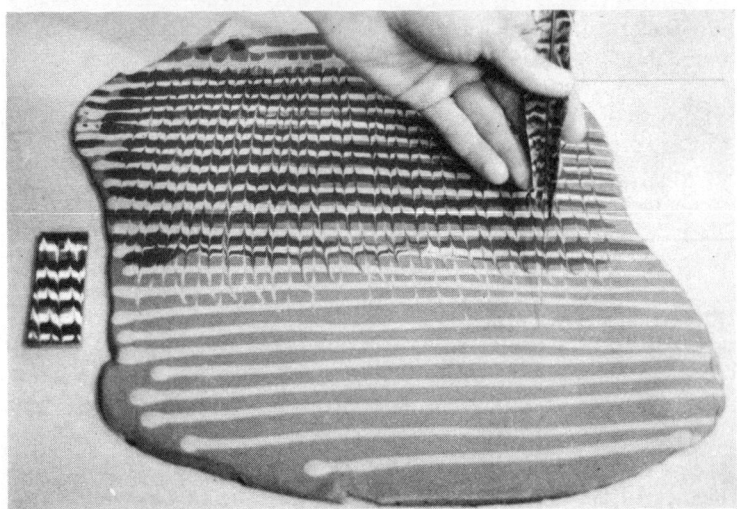

Figure 9.4   Feathering

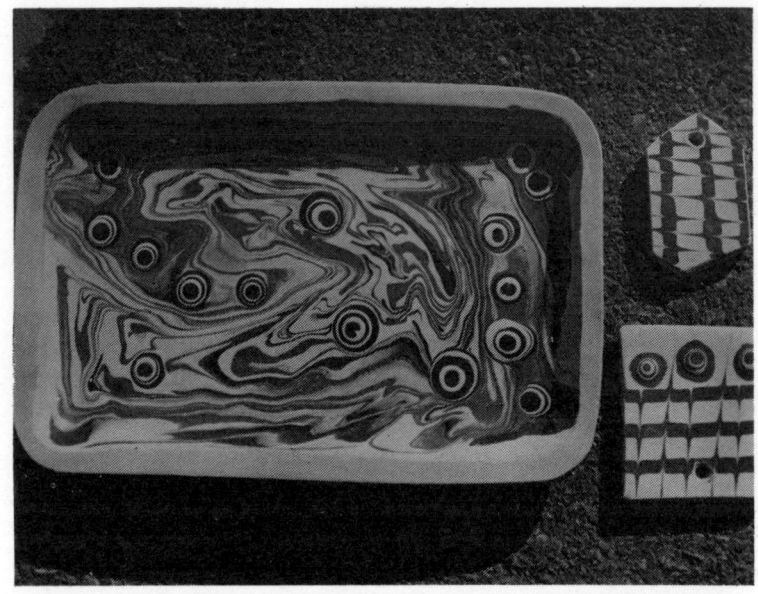

Figure 9.5   Marbling – marbled slip in a press-moulded dish with 'bull's eyes' patterns made with a slip-trailer. Also two simple pendants made from selected feathered and marbled slabs – these are cut when the clay is leather hard

MARBLING

A slab is covered with slip. While this is still wet, contrasting slip is dripped on at random from a brush or a trailer. When the slab is tilted or agitated (still on its board) the slips will 'marble'. Careful use of a slip trailer can produce concentric 'bull's eye' effects (figure 9.5) as one slip is dropped into the centre of another.

STENCIL

Cut or torn paper shapes can be used to resist chosen areas as a piece of work is dipped in slip, or when slip is brushed on (figure 9.6). You can either lay on damp paper shapes, which are carefully removed after the slip is applied, or apply the slip through windows cut out of the paper.

ENCAUSTIC OR INLAYING

When the form is leather hard, shallow recesses are carved into the surface with a looped wire tool or a suitable instrument such as a scoop-shaped lino cutting tool (figure 9.7a). Then contrasting slip (or soft clay) is inlaid, filling the recesses (figure 9.7b), and later, when any excess slip is scraped away, the design is revealed (figure 9.7c). Medieval floor-tiles were often made in this way and can still be seen in many ecclesiastical buildings.

40

Figure 9.6   Stencil – removing cut paper shapes which have been used to resist the coating of contrasting slip

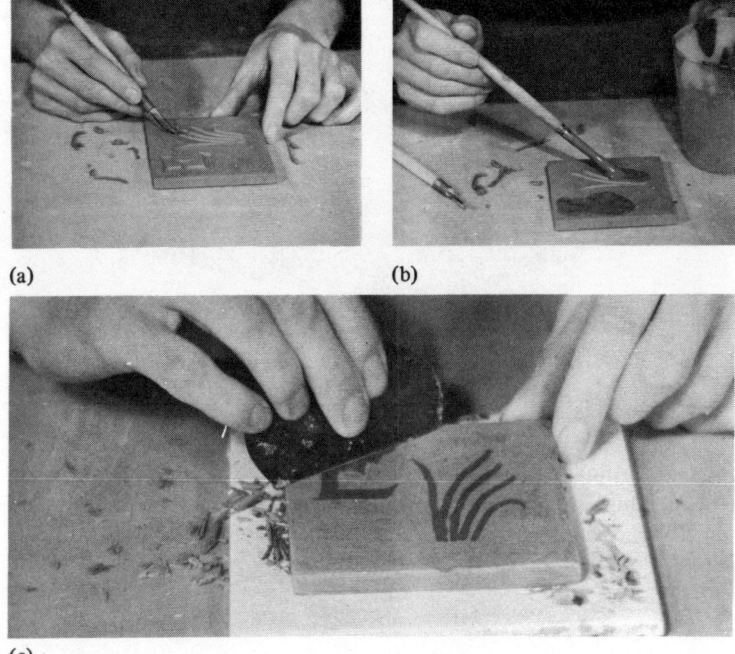

(a)   (b)

(c)

Figure 9.7   (a) Encaustic or inlaying – carving recesses with a looped wire
tool
(b) Filling the recesses with slip (soft clay can be used)
(c) Later scraping away the excess slip to reveal the inlayed
design

Figure 9.8   Small earthenware bottle with inlay, dated 1789, initials I. F.
(courtesy of the Hampshire Museum Service)

Dish shapes can be made from slip-covered slabs. When the surface is sufficiently dry but the body still fairly plastic, the slab is draped over a hump mould and then trimmed. Marbling can be done in pressed dishes. Selected parts of slip-decorated slabs can be used to make simple jewellery, if they are cut before the slabs are too dry and brittle.

10

Throwing

The technique of *throwing* is fairly complex and any written descrip-
tion is bound to be somewhat inadequate. A great deal of practice and
experience is necessary before all the skills and their application can
be accomplished. However, it is well worth time and effort, for in the
long run the very act of throwing — its immediacy, its freshness and
vitality — is most rewarding. First it is essential that the clay be well
prepared. It must be freshly wedged or kneaded and should be of a
perfectly homogeneous, soft consistency. For the beginner, I would
suggest preparing a mass of clay from which a number of balls weighing about 0.7 kg (1.5 lb) can be made. A jug of water, a soft sponge or
chamois leather, a wire-cutter and a turning tool will be required, and
these should be arranged in or near the wheel tray. The potter's wheel
should preferably be clean and the wheel head damp (not wet). A ball
of clay is slapped on to the middle of the wheel head. Usually electrically powered wheels revolve anti-clockwise and a kick-wheel
should be set in motion in this direction (left-handed people may
prefer to work clockwise — transposing the following directions).

There are three stages to go through before the cylinder or bowl is
formed: *centring, coning* and *opening out*.

Centring (figure 10.1) is the technique of forcing and controlling
the spinning clay so that it is perfectly true and concentric. Water is

Figure 10.1   Centring — applying an inward pressure using the weight of the
body through the left arm, and a downward pressure with the right
hand

splashed on to the clay and almost every time the hands approach the clay they should first be dipped in the water to provide lubrication. Two pressures are used to force the spinning clay to the centre of the wheel — inwards and downwards. There are various ways of doing this, but in general it is worth remembering that it is more efficient to use the weight of the body, through the shoulders and arms, rather than arm muscles and wrists alone. One method is to lock the left elbow to the hip and to lean on the clay. The weight of the body is transferred through the straight arm, and the palm of the left hand forces the clay on to the centre while the right palm presses downwards. Another method, suitable for small amounts of clay, is to place the right hand over and around the back of the clay, with the left hand over the right. A downward and inward pressure will then produce a centred dome shape. It is important not to release pressure suddenly because this will send the clay off centre again. Centring may take some time to master, so don't despair if the clay seems reluctant to stay in the middle.

Coning (figure 10.2) the centred clay will promote mixing and will render the clay more responsive. This is done by squeezing the clay from either side with both palms. This forces the clay up into a conical shape. It is then pressed down with the right palm and in with the left. This is repeated two or three times. Centring and coning can be carried out simultaneously, with practice. When centred, there should be no trace of lateral wobble whatsoever.

The initial *opening* is made with the right thumb after steadying the right arm on the wheel tray and the hand on the wheel head. The thumb finds the top dead centre and then is steadily, but firmly pressed down in the clay, stopping about 12–19 mm (½–¾ in.) from the wheel head. Again it is important not to exert or release pressure suddenly. Water is splashed into the opening and the thumb is again used to open out the clay inside.

Now the throwing or raising of the walls is carried out. There are basically two shapes — the cylinder and the bowl — and you should really decide which you wish to make. The cylinder, which offers a basis for exploring great variation in form, requires the clay to be opened out, flat and wide on the inside (figure 10.3). This is important, otherwise the clay cannot really be pulled up effectively and the shape will remain too thick in the lower half. To do this, the right thumb is drawn out flat, as if trying to touch the palm. The bowl, on the other hand, needs a curved inside and so the thumb is drawn out and upwards at the same time.

Throwing is the action of raising up and thinning the spinning clay wall, and here again there is a variety of approach, but the following is a popular method. Working at 'a quarter past three' the first and middle fingers of the left hand are placed inside the opened-out shape. The corresponding fingers of the right hand, or more efficiently, the crooked knuckle of the right index finger, are now used to squeeze,

Figure 10.2 Coning — thoroughly mixing the clay to create a responsive consistency, with an inward and upward pressure

Figure 10.3 Opening out

Figure 10.4 'Knuckling up' — raising the walls of a cylinder. Note how the thumb of the left hand serves to link with the right hand

Figure 10.5 Opening out a bowl shape

coax and pull the clay wall, starting at the bottom, up into a thinner wall of regular thickness (figure 10.4). For a cylinder an inward pressure is necessary to 'contain' the shape, otherwise it may flair out as a result of centrifugal force from the spinning wheel. Slowing the wheel down as the form becomes thinner is helpful. A bowl is made by pulling the wall up and out (figure 10.5). The inside can be shaped and smoothed to a flowing curve with a sponge, but an excess of clay needs to be left on the outside to support the shape. This is later turned off.

Figure 10.6 Refining a rim with a soft natural sponge

Figure 10.7 Trimming away excess clay with a triangular turning tool

Figure 10.8 Forming a pouring lip on a jug

Figure 10.9 Making a 'throat' for the jug

Figure 10.10 Releasing a form from the wheel head

Should there be a tendency for the rim of the pot to become thin and ragged, it will need to be carefully rounded off with your fingers or with a sponge (figure 10.6) or chamois leather. By allowing the rim to spin through the thumb and finger of the left hand, the right middle finger can gently compress and round off the edge.

When the piece is finished, any clay which has spread out on to the wheel can be cleaned off with a turning tool (figure 10.7), and any excess thickness (not from bowls) can be trimmed away. A thin wire, held taut, is drawn under the pot (figure 10.10). Water splashed on to the wheel will be drawn under when the wire is taken through again, and the form can be gently pushed on to a suitable tile or bat. Glazed tiles may be used (figure 10.11) but the pot should be removed at the leather-hard stage before it sticks. Large pots are better thrown on thin, round bats (figure 10.12), stuck down on the wheel head with clay, and these are removed along with the thrown form.

Figure 10.11 Pushing a thrown bowl on to a glazed tile (*Note* This should be removed before it dries and sticks)

Figure 10.12 Placing a round bat on the wheel for throwing a large form. A pad of clay is first thrown on the wheel and is then scored with the point of a turning tool. This enables a large, heavy form to be removed, complete with bat, so avoiding distortion and damage

Figure 10.13 Collaring – narrowing the top of a cylinder

Figure 10.14 Thrown pot with 'gourded' indentations, stoneware – Malcolm
Pepper

49

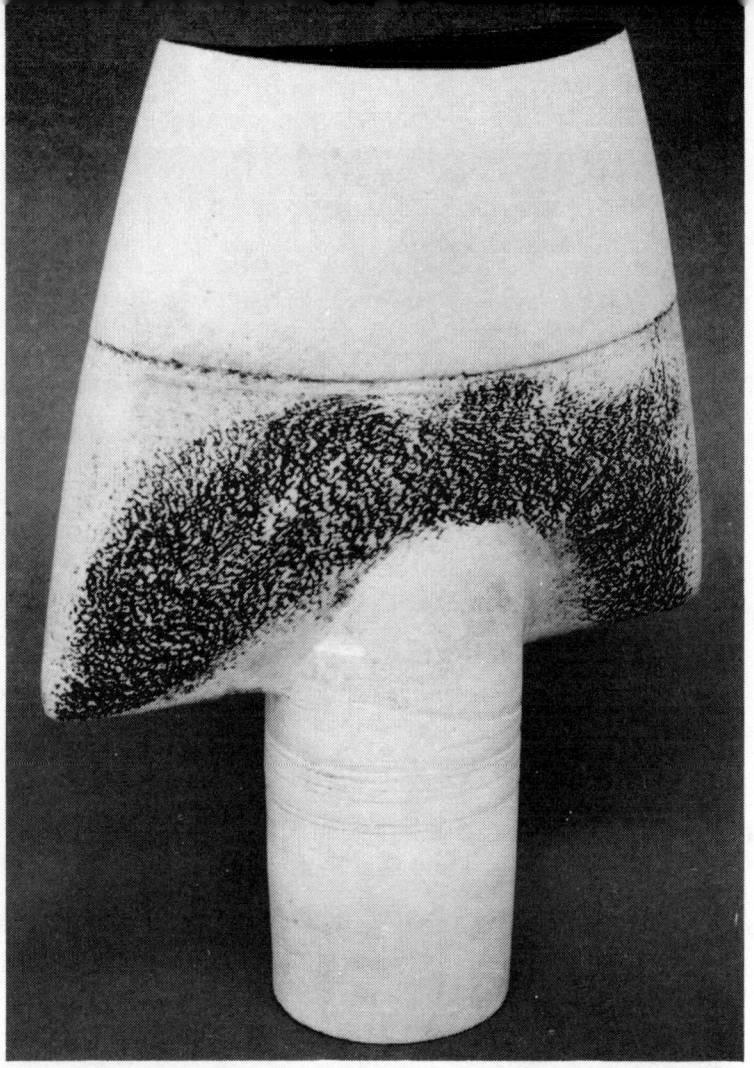

Figure 10.15 Vase, made from two thrown forms, stoneware – Hans Coper
(courtesy of the Hampshire Museum Service)

Variations in the thrown form are virtually endless. 'Bellies' and
'shoulders' can be formed by gently pushing out with the left fingers
while the right hand controls and counters on the outside. 'Waists' and
'necks' are made by collaring the form between the hands or fingers
(figure 10.13). Narrow necks are made with a combination of throwing, using one finger inside, and collaring between the fingers. Lips for
pouring are made while the clay is still wet (see figures 10.8 and 10.9).

Tall forms can be made by throwing cylinders of equal diameter,
which are joined when leather hard. Lids and spouts are made not by
centring very small balls of clay, but by throwing on the top of a
large, centred mass. Numerous small shapes can be thrown this way,
each one being cut off before the top of the clay is centred for the
next.

11

Turning

When leather hard, thrown forms can be finished off by trimming or turning. This is not always necessary if the piece was 'completed' and regular in section in the throwing stage, but it is often the case with bowls where the clay, left to support the outward-flowing shape, needs to be turned away to leave a foot (figures 11.1, 11.2 and 11.3). Some types of lid are completed in the same way; the excess clay is turned away to leave a knob.

Figure 11.1 Marking grooves for a foot ring with the point of a turning tool. The leather-hard bowl is held in place with pads of clay, thumbed on to the wheel

Figure 11.2 Shaving away excess clay with the edge of the tool

Figure 11.3 Finishing the foot with a bevelled edge by holding the turning tool
at an angle

It is important that the form be leather hard — that is, firm enough
to support itself without distorting when inverted on the wheel, yet
still damp enough to turn away cleanly without chipping, By feeling
the walls between thumb and finger, you should be able to assess how
much clay needs to be turned off.

Turning-tools come in a variety of shapes and sizes. The more
common types are of flat steel with a bevelled-edge blade, often triangular, bent at a right angle to the handle. Others are of looped, flat
wire set in a wooden handle.

Simple shapes, such as cylinders and bowls, are first carefully
centred on a damp wheel and then held in place with plastic clay
which is thumbed down on to the wheel head. Narrow-necked forms
or those with inward-sloping rims may need to be supported inside
with plastic clay thrown to size, or may be better held in a suitable
pot or a specially thrown ring of clay (figure 11.4). Large bowls which
are wider than the wheel head can be supported on top of another pot
or a hump of centred clay.

Working at a fairly slow speed, the tool is held firmly with the arms
braced on the wheel tray or against the body. Working from the
centre out to a 'quarter past three', light incisions can be made with
the pointed part of the tool and the clay is removed with the edge. If
the clay is leather hard, it should come away rather like curly wood
shavings.

Figure 11.4   How to support a narrow-necked pot for turning

A foot, turned from the excess clay on the bowl, will often add
finesse and elegance. A certain amount of shaping to the outside can
be done — a flowing curve can be formed following that on the inside.
Proportion of foot to rim is something that you will be able to judge
with experience. If it is too wide, a bowl will appear squat and lifeless;
if too narrow, then it may not properly support the bowl. From a
practical point of view, a turned foot is a great aid to glazing in that it
allows a pot to be gripped when dipping.

12

Handles, lids and spouts

HANDLES

Vessels which require handles are varied and, because making methods, functions and styles also vary, it is difficult to give any general directions except to say that a badly designed handle will neither look right nor perform comfortably.

A slab-built vessel, such as a cylindrical coffee mug, will require a simple handle, in keeping with its straight-sided nature. Such a handle can be made from a strip of clay cut from a slab and applied with slip. The sharp edges should be smoothed off with a damp sponge. A similar handle can be made from a coil, which is gently patted or smoothed down with a damp sponge to a flat, oval section. A round coil will rarely look right; it will appear crude and heavy, but a flattish oval handle will have both strength and visual compatibility.

Thrown vessels, such as mugs, jugs and teapots, need 'pulled' handles. A pulled handle has the same fresh character as the thrown

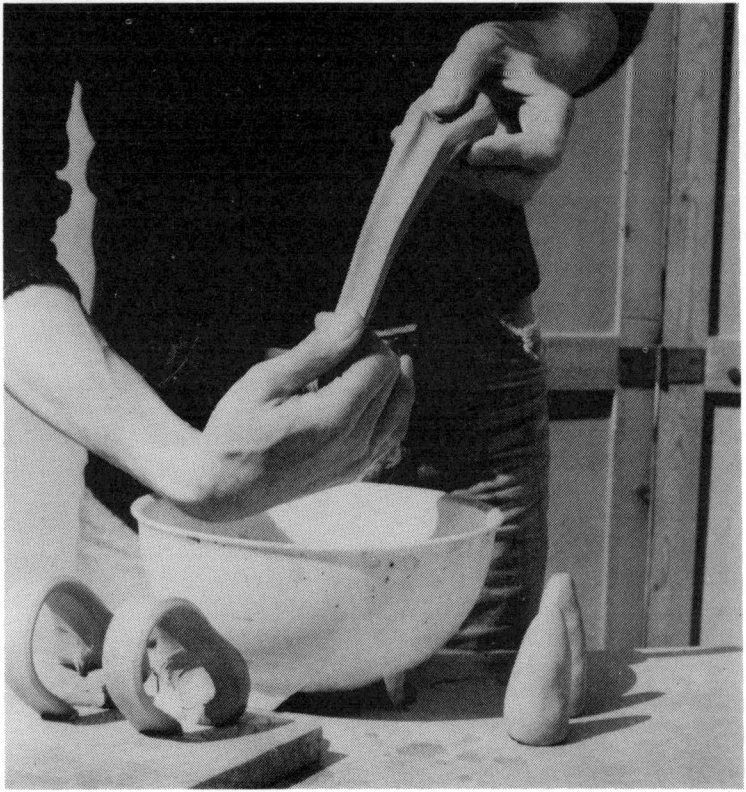

Figure 12.1 Pulling a handle

form and, if attached in a sympathetic manner, will become an integral part of the pot; it will look as if it is 'growing out' of the pot rather than just stuck on. To make pulled handles (figure 12.1), first prepare some plastic clay and make tapering cone shapes, like carrots. By holding the thick end of the carrot in one hand, the other hand, constantly lubricated with water, gently coaxes, extrudes and extends the clay to form a long, flat shape. The way in which the pulling hand is held during this operation will determine the shape and character of the handle. Large, vigorous handles can have a deep, sweeping groove fashioned by the thumb. Small handles can be pulled through a clenched fist and will have fluid lines which may correspond to the throwing rings on a pot. Pulling handles does take some time to master and, as with throwing, well prepared clay and plenty of lubrication are vital.

Pulled handles should be left, preferably standing in a looped position, until they can be touched without damage. Then the required length is cut or pinched off the thick end of the carrot and attached to the pot (figure 12.2). The pot should be in the same state as the handle — that is, prior to leather hard. If the handle tapers slightly, then it is usual to attach the thicker end first, in the higher position, to the keyed and slipped surface of the pot. Then the handle can be 'sighted' and the excess length pinched off before the lower end is joined. A brisk thumbing in (figure 12.3) of this lower end is popular with studio potters and is reminiscent of medieval tankards and jugs. An uninterrupted curved shape should be sought, one which does not extend higher than the top lip of the pot, which may then be damaged when the pot is inverted. Sections of pulled handles are commonly used to make lugs on casseroles, applied in a horizontal curve. They can also be used to make matching knobs on lids.

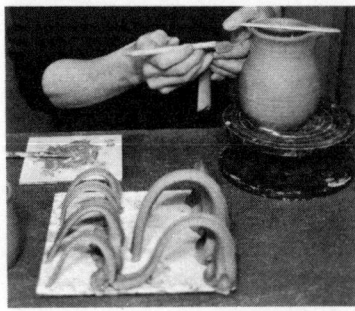 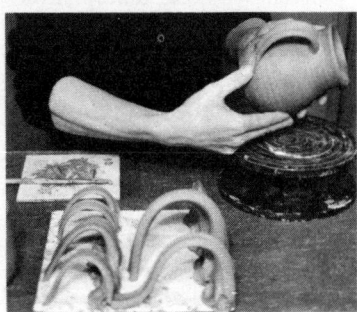

Figure 12.2 Fixing a handle to a jug with other pulled handles drying out. Note that the handle is being keyed and that a modelling tool is laid across the jug to help position the handle opposite the pouring lip

Figure 12.3 Thumbing in the handle

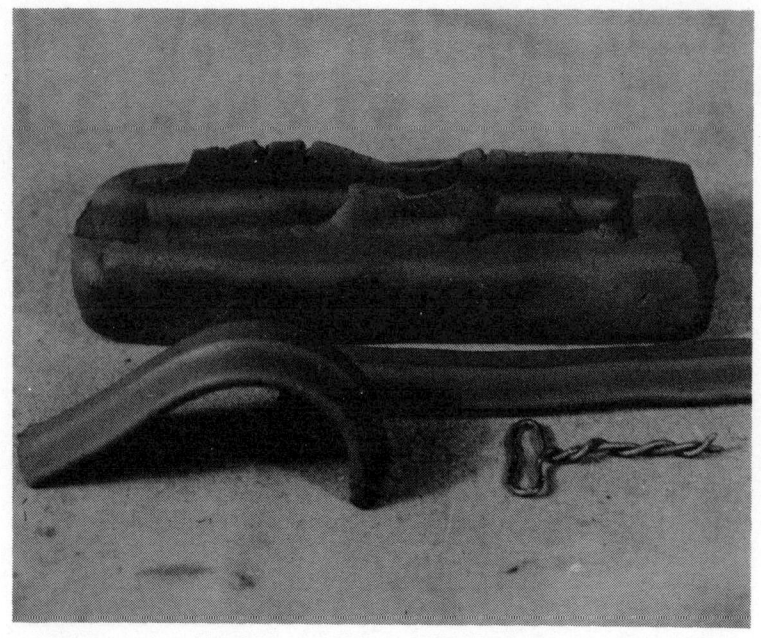

Figure 12.4   Handles produced from a block of clay with a looped wire tool

Another way of making handles to suit thrown forms is to use a looped wire tool, bent to the desired shape. When this tool is drawn through the plastic clay, it will produce a strip which can be used to make a handle almost as fresh looking as a pulled one (figure 12.4).

Handles can also be made from thrown shapes which are applied in the same way as saucepan handles. Teapots can have cane handles which span the top of the form. These can be bought from pottery suppliers and lugs are made for their attachment at the making stage.

Although there is scope for experiment, tradition is probably the best guide in the long run.

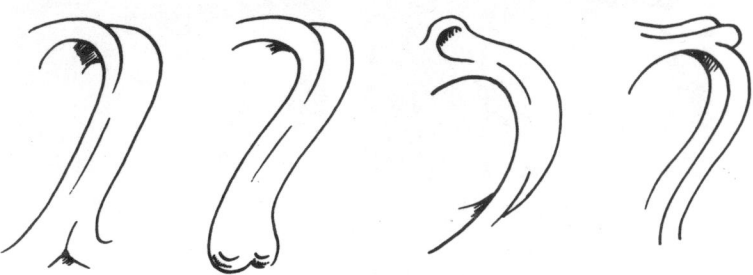

Figure 12.5   Handle styles – some variation in 'conclusions' and thumb-stops

Figure 12.6   Three thrown jugs with pulled handles — stoneware

LIDS

A pot requiring a lid will sometimes need a small ledge, called a gallery, just inside the top edge. This is made on a thrown pot by carefully pushing a little clay down from the rim with a square tool as the pot revolves (figure 12.8). A modelling tool can be modified for this purpose, or the handle of a turning tool may be used. The inside diameter of the top of the pot is measured with callipers before the pot dries and shrinks.

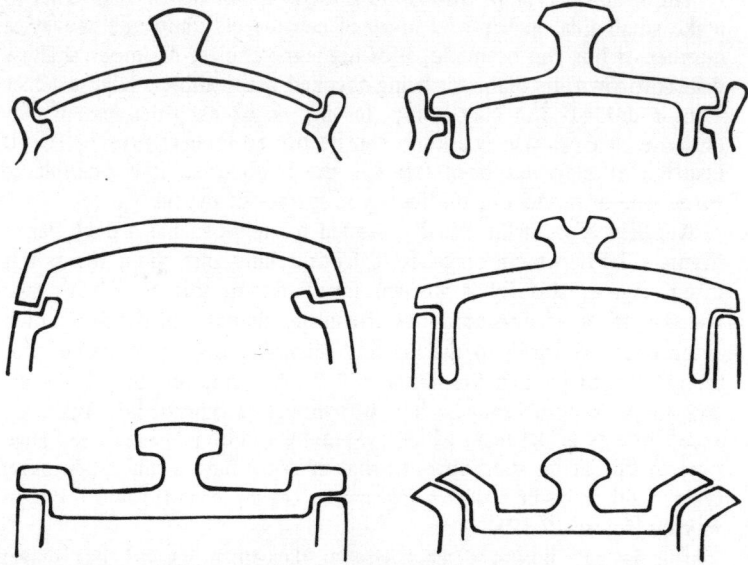

Figure 12.7   Types of lid — the top four are thrown upside-down with the knobs turned or added later; the bottom two are thrown the right way up

Figure 12.8 Making a gallery, using the square handle on a turning tool

The simplest type of thrown lid is made upside-down. It is easier to make small lids on top of a lump of centred clay and in this way, a number of lids can be made, allowing some choice. A simple, shallow dish is thrown, its diameter being checked with callipers (figure 12.9). This is cut off the clay hump, leaving an excess thickness of clay underneath from which a knob can be turned later (figure 12.10). If insufficient clay has been left for the knob, then it is possible to throw one or model one on the keyed surface of the lid.

Another type of lid, usually needed for teapots, has a deep flange (figure 12.11) which prevents it from falling out when the pot is tilted. Again, this lid is thrown upside-down, this time with two measurements to consider: first, the inside diameter of the pot, which determines the width of the lid, and secondly, the inside diameter of the gallery into which the flange will fit. A square tool may be necessary to perfect the shape when throwing this type of lid. Again, an excess of clay is left from which eventually a knob is made. The flange type of lid can be used on a pot that does not have a gallery. Another type of lid, suitable for a storage jar or casserole, is thrown the right way up (figure 12.12).

For slabbed, lidded forms, the same rules apply, except that flanges are made from strips of clay or coils, and that even though all the work should be done when the clay is leather hard, some allowance should be made for shrinkage and distortion.

Figure 12.9 Checking the diameter of a simple lid, thrown upside-down

Figure 12.10 Turning away excess clay to make a knob

Figure 12.11 Throwing a flange type of lid, upside-down

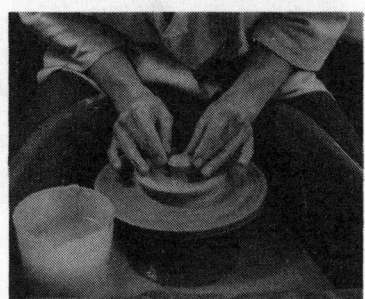

Figure 12.12 Throwing a lid

Figure 12.13 A casserole with a choice of lids – one lid has a turned knob, the other has a strap-type knob made from a section of 'pulled' clay to match the lugs

Figure 12.14 Collaring a small cylinder to make a spout

SPOUTS

The pouring lip of a thrown jug is made directly after the piece has been thrown. This is done by supporting the rim between thumb and finger of one hand and carefully pulling and smoothing out with the thumb or finger of the other hand (see figures 10.8 and 10.9).

A spout, such as that required for a teapot, is made from a small thrown cylinder, collared to a conical shape (figure 12.14). A number of spouts can be made from one piece of centred clay and will allow some choice. When leather hard, the spout can be cut to fit the pot, often with a double curvature to consider. This is done in slow stages, offering up the spout until a good fit and position are obtained. The tip of the spout should be just below the top rim of the pot. Before finally joining the spout with slip, perforations are made in the body of the pot.

It may be noticed that with some clays, the spout, after drying and firing, appears to have twisted. This is known as *torque reaction*. What happens is that during the throwing and collaring on an anti-clockwise wheel, a clockwise twisting pressure is imparted to the spout. On drying and firing, this clockwise twisting actually continues so that it may be necessary to counter this reaction by applying the spout in such a way that when the torque reaction occurs, the spout will straighten up — that is, when looking at the teapot from the front, the top of the spout should have an incline down to the left so that on twisting clockwise it will align with the top of the pot.

TEAPOT PROJECT

Making a teapot is a good way of applying wheel skills. It involves, first of all, design with functional and aesthetic considerations, and then all the component parts must be made and joined in the right sequence. (See figures 12.15a to f.) The planning and timing of all the operations are critical, especially if you are attending a weekly course. Here is a suggested plan which will probably involve the use of a damp cupboard between stages, and possibly the need to speed up the drying of some components by placing them on a kiln or near a heater.

(1) Body of teapot thrown (developed from a cylinder, rotund in character). Gallery formed. Opening and gallery measured with callipers.

(2) Two or three lids thrown (with flange) from one piece of centred clay, with the aid of calliper measurement.

(3) Two or three spouts thrown from one piece of clay.

(4) Two or three handles pulled.

(5) Before leather hard, teapot foot turned.

(6) Before too hard, spout selected, cut to shape and offered up, perforations made and spout luted on with possible allowance for twist.

(7) Handle selected and applied opposite spout or lugs, modelled on for Oriental-type cane handle.

(8) Lid turned down to make knob, or knob thrown or modelled on.

Figure 12.15 Teapot   (a)   Cutting a spout

61

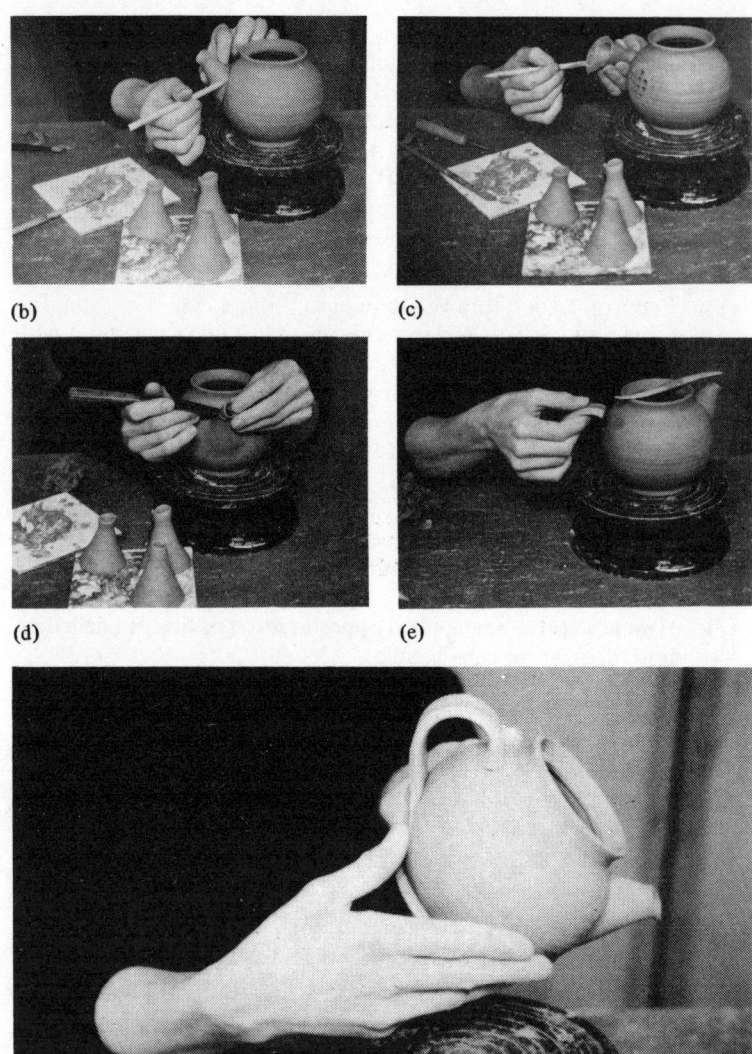

(b)

(c)

(d)

(e)

(f)

Figure 12.15 (b) Marking the desired position of the spout so that perforations can be made

(c) Keying the spout – note the perforations, made with a special hollow tool and the keyed surface surrounding them

(d) Fettling the spout with an allowance made for twisting

(e) Fixing the handle

(f) Thumbing in the handle

62

Figure 12.16 Teapots with cane handles attached to lugs

13

Kilns and biscuit-firing

Figure 13.1   A biscuit firing – note how the work is stacked

When finished work is completely dry – and this may take many days or even weeks – it is slowly heated in a kiln. This first firing, or biscuit firing, changes the clay chemically and irreversibly to form pottery. Some studio potters, for reasons of economy, miss out the biscuit firing and glaze the green ware, but this has drawbacks because the ware is very fragile and so glazing requires great expertise. The normal procedure then is to have two firings, biscuit and glaze.

In the biscuit firing, pieces can be packed one on top of another, with heavier work at the bottom of the kiln (figure 13.1). Small pieces can be placed inside larger ones, as long as allowance is made for shrinkage which may cause one piece to be trapped inside another. Kiln furniture may sometimes have to be used to ensure that the firing chamber is filled economically, especially if the firing includes a number of delicate or irregularly shaped forms which cannot be stacked safely.

Electric kilns are the most common, but gas, oil and sometimes wood-burning types may be encountered. Whatever type of kiln is used for biscuit firing, the temperature must be controlled so that the firing progresses slowly. If clay is damp, or if it is heated too quickly, it will shatter as water, turning to steam, tries to escape.

There is a variety of equipment used for controlling electric kilns, varying from simple 'low, medium, high' switches to sophisticated programme controllers. A common fitment is a *simmerstat* which has a dial calibrated from 0 to 100. This can be set to control the flow of power to the kiln for chosen periods. For example, set at 25, the simmerstat will regulate power to the kiln for 25 per cent of the time.

In a biscuit firing, the bung is removed to ventilate the kiln and to allow moisture to escape, and the heat is built up slowly to about 300 $^{\circ}$C (low or 25 per cent). During this period, the free water is lost Then the kiln can be switched up to 'medium', or 50 per cent, for a few hours. Above about 600 $^{\circ}$C, the chemically combined water in the clay will be driven off, and the bung can be replaced and the kiln switched up to 'high', or 100 per cent. The usual maximum temperature for a biscuit firing is about 1000 $^{\circ}$C. This means that most clays will still be very porous, the water having been driven off to leave millions of minute pockets of air. This porosity is a great aid to glaze application. When the maximum temperature has been reached, the kiln is switched off and allowed to cool slowly. The bung can be removed in the latter stages of cooling but the door should not be opened before 100 $^{\circ}$C.

Temperature is recorded on a *pyrometer* but if none is fitted, small pyrometric cones are used to register heat/work. These bend at prescribed temperatures, denoted by a number impressed in the cone, and they are placed inside the kiln, close to the peep-hole. Some kilns have a *kiln sitter*, a device which uses the shrinking of a pyrometric cone to trigger off the switch.

14

Glaze

Glaze is a glass-like covering and its purpose is primarily to make pottery waterproof, durable and hygienic in use. It is also important to the finished appearance of a piece of work, being a decorative source of colour, 'feel' and texture. Glaze formulation is a highly specialised field but, fortunately, simple glaze recipes and materials are generally available, as are commercially produced, ready-made glazes, for use in schools and colleges.

A glaze is normally described by its maturing temperature (for example, earthenware, stoneware), then perhaps by its predominant colour or surface characteristic (for example, white, opaque, oatmeal, matt, glossy). Sometimes a glaze may be named after a particular ingredient (for example, ash, tin, limestone).

The main element in a glaze is *silica*, a natural glass-forming material. This is often introduced in the form of flint or quartz.

The second element is a *flux*, to lower the melting point of the silica and to cause the ingredients to melt and fuse. This can be found in feldspar, whiting (chalk) and borax, for example.

A third element is required to balance the other two and to help them to adhere to the side of a pot. This is *alumina*, one source of which is clay.

Notice how these materials are closely related to clay itself. In fact it could be said that certain glazes, especially high-temperature ones, are composed of finely crushed rocks, related to the ones that originally decomposed and weathered to form clay.

EARTHENWARE GLAZE

Low-temperature pottery requires the use of glazes with powerful fluxes. Lead (not now widely used in education establishments) and borax, two such fluxes, are unsuitable in their raw state because they are highly toxic and soluble, being difficult to mix with the other ingredients in suspension. so base glazes can be made from *frits*. Frits are produced commercially by making these soluble elements plus silica into a glass. This is then cooled and crushed to a fine powder — a frit — which is then of low solubility and therefore easier to mix and safer to use when added to water to make the raw glaze.

STONEWARE GLAZE

High-temperature glazes often use feldspar as a base material because it naturally and conveniently contains the basic glaze requirements in the right proportions. So this cheap, common rock, feldspar — the original source of clay — when crushed to a powder, will make a stoneware glaze.

Another basis for stoneware glaze is wood ash. This contains alumina and silica and various other minerals, depending on the type of wood and the soil in which the tree grew. Ash from a wood fire can be washed in water and sieved to remove impurities such as charcoal. However, too much washing may remove certain important soluble materials. Neither feldspar nor ash on their own will produce perfect glazes, but it is possible to combine them and to experiment with various changes in proportion, starting with, say, 50/50 by dry weight and taking care to note all experiments. Other starting points in basic glaze experiments can be the adding of materials such as powdered clay and whiting (chalk) to feldspar as secondary fluxes, to help the feldspar melt and fuse.

GLAZE MODIFICATION

Opaque Glaze
Transparent, glossy glazes can be made white and opaque with the addition of certain opacifiers, commonly oxides of tin, zirconium and titanium.

Matt Glaze
Materials such as zinc, talc and whiting are used to produce matt or semi-matt glazes. Whiting is a common secondary flux in stoneware glaze, but if sufficient quantity is used, will also produce a matt surface.

Glaze Experiments
Many adult education pottery courses use ready-made glazes because, owing to the shortage of time, space and equipment, they are easy to use and reliable. It may still be possible for you to make simple glaze experiments by making modifications to a basic glaze in use. If there is a simple transparent glaze or an opaque glaze you can try making matt or semi-matt glazes by adding percentages of talc, zinc or whiting. Do this by weighing out, say, 100 g of the dry glaze then adding, say, 5 per cent of the matting agent. Then proceed to add a larger percentage, and so on. Records should be kept of all experiments, and the glaze is best applied to small tiles or preferably tiny bowls which will enable you to see how the glaze alters in appearance and covering ability on the sides, edges and bottom of the bowl.

Similar experiments can be carried out to make coloured glazes, using the oxides described in chapter 15, or commercially produced glaze stains.

GLAZE APPLICATION
Glaze, whether mixed from a recipe or bought ready-made, is mixed with water until it is the consistency of thin cream (approximately 0.5 kg to 0.5 litres (17.5 oz to 1 pint) and then sieved through a fine mesh lawn (120 mesh). Water acts as the vehicle for applying the glaze to the porous biscuit form. Glaze should be kept in a lidded con-

tainer and, because it is in suspension, must be thoroughly stirred before use. It is advisable to use a stick for this purpose. You must be positive about glaze application. The biscuit form is very porous and any hesitancy when glazing may result in uneven or too thick an application. The following are the usual methods of applying glaze.

Dipping
Small forms can be totally or partially submerged in the glaze. If the whole piece is to be covered, it is held between thumb and finger, and after dipping it is quickly but carefully withdrawn and allowed to dry off before being stood upright. This usually takes only a few seconds because the water quickly soaks into the porous body, leaving a coating of powdered raw glaze on the surface. Any bare patch left by the finger, say, on the rim, can be glazed by quickly dabbing a little glaze on with the finger or a soft brush. This needs to be done carefully because any attempt to 'paint' the glaze on may in fact dislodge more glaze. Any runs which appear on the surface can be gently removed with your finger nail or a suitable tool. When dipping stoneware it is necessary to leave the base free of glaze, and very often it is possible to grip the base of the form and dip in up to about 12.5 mm (½ in.) from the foot, or up to some suitable place on the pot (figure 14.1). This usually means that there is no problem with bare patches on the rim. If stoneware is totally submerged, perhaps because it cannot be gripped at the base, then it is important to scrape and wipe all glaze clear of the base and from a little way up the sides in case the glaze runs and sticks the piece to the kiln shelf. Earthenware may be left glazed underneath, and stilts are used to support it in the kiln.

Figure 14.1   Glazing the inside of a bowl – pouring out the glaze with a twisting movement to ensure full coverage

Pouring

Small quantities of glaze can be poured over a form (figure 14.2). This is also useful for glazing the inside of a bowl, when the glaze is quickly poured out again, using a twisting movement to ensure full covering inside before dipping the outside (figure 14.3). Random pouring or dripping of different glazes can be effective; so can the dipping of one glaze over another, when the glazes may react with each other to produce interesting colours and textures.

Figure 14.2 Pouring glaze over a tall pot, using a turning action of the wrist to ensure full coverage

Figure 14.3 Dipping the bowl to glaze the outside — this is a stoneware glaze so the foot of the bowl is left unglazed

Brushing

Small forms can be glazed with a soft brush. This is usually unsatisfactory with larger forms because the covering will be uneven, but it is useful if it is desired to glaze only certain areas of a form.

Spraying

Glaze can be sprayed through an air gun. Blending of different glazes can be effected, but without proper air-extraction facilities, the method is unhealthy.

Care should always be exercised when glazing. Any spillage should be immediately wiped up with a damp sponge before the glaze dries and gets into the atmosphere, since prolonged exposure to such conditions can cause respiratory disease. Lids should always be replaced on glaze containers directly after use, and you should wash your hands and clean your fingernails with a nail brush as soon as possible after glazing.

BASIC GLAZE RECIPES

*Earthenware Transparent** 1020–1150 °C
   Borax frit 90 parts
   China clay 10 parts

*Earthenware White Opaque** 1020–1150 °C
   As above, plus 12 parts zircon or 7 parts tin oxide

*Earthenware White Matt** 1020–1150 °C
   As above white opaque, plus 18 parts zinc oxide and 4 parts titanium dioxide

*Stoneware Ash Semi Matt** 1260 °C
   Feldspar 40 parts
   Ash 40 parts
   Ball clay 20 parts

Stoneware Transparent†
   Feldspar 70 parts
   Whiting 12.5 parts
   China clay 13 parts
   Flint 4.5 parts

* Harry Fraser, *Glazes for the Craft Potter* (Pitman, London, 1976).
† David Hamilton, *Manual of Pottery and Ceramics* (Thames & Hudson, London, 1974).

15

Colour

Naturally occurring metallic deposits will give clay certain colour characteristics. Metals in the form of oxides are also used to introduce colour into clays, slips and glazes and are also used as pigments in surface decoration. It is interesting to note that different kiln-firing conditions will produce different results. Electric kilns usually have a clean, bright, oxygen-burning atmosphere (oxidation) which produces the colours expected of oxides. With gas, oil and solid-fuel fired kilns, it is possible to alter combustion and cut off or 'reduce' the amount of oxygen consumed (reduction). In a reduction atmosphere, which is usually smoky, the fire will extract oxygen from wherever it can, including any metal substances in the clay or glaze. A different colour response, this time related to the metal rather than its oxide, will be seen under reduced conditions.

For a studio potter, the following are the most commonly used oxides.

Oxide	Raw Colour	Effect	Percentage Use
Iron	Red or black	Yellows, red-browns, black (greys in reduction)	1–10
Cobalt	Black	Blue, black	0.2–2
Copper	Green or black	Turquoise, greens, black (reds in reduction)	1–5
Manganese	Black	'Purple'-browns, black	1–10
Chromium	Green	Greens (hard and dull), pinks if used with tin oxide	1–3

This is only a generalised table of effects. Reactions will vary not only according to the percentage added to a slip or glaze but also to clays, glazes used and kiln atmosphere. It should be noted that cobalt is very strong and should be used with care. Too much cobalt will produce unpleasant 'inky' blacks. There are many other oxides but their use is limited, especially in educational establishments, owing to their very toxic nature and/or high cost — for example, cadmium, a source of red.

Figure 15.1 Thrown vase, stoneware 'agate' ware – Lucie Rie (courtesy of the Portsmoth Museum and Art Gallery)

Figure 15.2 'Towards a Third Dimension', earthenware with painted pigment – Liz Fritch (courtesy of the Portsmouth Museum and Art Gallery)

Figure 15.3 Agate bowl on base, stoneware – Gordon Baldwin (courtesy of the Portsmouth Museum and Art Gallery)

Body stains, glaze stains, underglaze and onglaze colours are compounded commercially from metal oxides to give a variety of colour options. However, although some of these may be fitting for certain types of work, they are not always suitable for hand-formed pots, many colours being garish or rather flat and synthetic in appearance. A bright yellow glaze can look very attractive on a slabbed form such as the 'telephone' (figure 19.6), but would be out of keeping with the earthy character of a robust coil pot.

MAKING COLOURED SLIPS AND GLAZES

Coloured slips and glazes can be made by weighing out quantities of the dry material (powdered clay or glaze) and then a percentage of oxide or stain. Suppliers of stains give percentage figures in their catalogues, but generally figures of 5 per cent addition in use with glaze and 10–15 per cent addition in use with slip are normal. Compared with their reaction in earthenware glazes, stains will produce less intense effects in stoneware.

To make a coloured slip
(1) Weigh a quantity of powdered clay — for example, 100 g.
(2) Add a percentage of stain — for example, 10 g.
(3) Stir in water until creamy.
(4) Sieve through an 80 or 100 mesh lawn.

To make a coloured glaze
(1) Weigh out a quantity of dry base glaze — for example, 100 g.
(2) Add a percentage of oxide/stain — for example, 5 g.
(3) Stir in water (approximately 0.5 litres to 0.5 kg) (1 pint to 16 oz).
(4) Sieve through a 120 mesh lawn.
(5) Stir and test for consistency by dipping a piece of biscuit shard. The glaze should dry off fairly quickly, leaving an even coating.

To make a coloured clay
Stains or oxides can be added to soft, fairly sticky clay during wedging or kneading. It is best to experiment with small quantities and have these fired and glazed, since the colour response is usually only seen to maximum effect after the glaze firing. Too much oxide may upset the chemical composition of the clay, acting as a flux and lowering the maturing temperature of the body. Small quantities of coloured clay can be made by drying out coloured slip on a plaster bat. When it is plastic it can be kneaded in the fingers.

By partially mixing clays of differing colours, it is possible to make *agate ware*. Pots thrown on a wheel with partially wedged clays will usually need to be shaved down with a turning tool at either the throwing or turning stages, to remove the coating of smudged slurry and to reveal the marbled patterns. Agate ware is glazed with a transparent glaze which brings out the colours to great effect.

Note   Some oxides are toxic in their raw state and should therefore be handled with care. Copper and cobalt should be used only for decorative effect and not on the surface of a pot which is to be used for food or drink, because certain food acids may attack the glazed surface and 'release' the toxic substance.

16

Decoration at the glazing stage

We have seen how the various ways of forming clay often suggest direction, shape and also surface quality. We have also looked at slip decoration. It may be, then, that a particular piece of work requires no more than a simple glaze (indeed, it may not even require that — terracotta is very attractive in its biscuit state and so are many stoneware clays when fired at stoneware temperature). 'Throwing rings' on a wheel-made pot will usually have sufficient visual interest and will even be emphasised by the way some glazes will settle in the depressions.

However, much can be done with the use of oxides and pigments derived from them, to decorate work at all stages of the ceramic process. Oxides can be used to change a clay body and to make a coloured slip. They can also be mixed with water and brushed on to the greenware prior to biscuit firing, but it is more common to decorate biscuit forms either before applying glaze, *underglaze*, or on top of the raw glaze prior to *glost* firing, *in-glaze*. The only problem with the underglaze method is that the oxide may be disturbed when glaze is applied, perhaps contaminating the glaze. The solution to this is to add a little gum arabic to the mixture of oxide and water to help adhesion. Proprietary underglaze colours may require a firing to harden them on before the glaze is applied. Oxides can be rubbed into previously scratched or carved recesses to emphasise the effect.

When decorating on top of the raw glaze, it should be remembered that the surface is really an absorbent powder and therefore any brush work will need to be quite free and spontaneous. Practice in handling a brush and knowledge of the strengths and effects of oxides can result in lively, unfussy decoration. Mixing the oxide with a little of the glaze used on the form will help in achieving an easily handled, paintable consistency. This is, in effect, brushing one glaze on top of another and will help the oxide to fuse into the glazed surface. A glazed tile can be used as a palette for preparing the mixture of pigment, water and/or glaze.

SOME COMMON DECORATIVE TECHNIQUES

Brushwork
Full, soft artist's-type brushes, or special Oriental caligraphic brushes which will 'point up', are best. They will hold enough pigment and with practice can produce an expressive range of flowing marks. A banding wheel can be used to apply lines around a regular form, and this can serve as a guide for free brush work (figures 16.1 and 16.2). Simple, rhythmic patterns usually work well, and a good brush can

produce a fitting effect when simply touched on and delicately withdrawn from the surface so that the point of the brush leaves a freely tapering mark.

Figure 16.1 Banding oxide on top of raw glaze

Figure 16.2 Free brush-work using the banded lines as a basis

Stipple
Mottled effects can be produced by applying oxides with a sponge (figure 16.3). Speckled effects can be 'sprayed' on with a short, stiff bristle brush, flicked with the finger (figure 16.4). This can be used with paper stencils to block out chosen areas.

Figure 16.3   Applying oxide with a sponge

Figure 16.4   'Spraying' oxide with a short bristled stencil brush

Wax Resist

Melted wax or a proprietary substitute can be used to resist glaze on chosen areas of a pot. In some iron-bearing clays this may have the effect of producing rich reds on unglazed areas. Wax can also be used to partially resist one glaze when applied over another. A certain amount of drying time will be necessary when doing this. After applying the first glaze, the form should be left for a few minutes, perhaps near a kiln or a heater until it feels dry. Then the wax is brushed on and allowed to dry. When the pot is dipped into the second glaze, it will not adhere to the wax surface and a characteristic 'broken' outline to the decorated area will result (figure 16.5). If a pot is inverted and carefully dipped into the second glaze, the air inside the pot will stop any glaze forming on the inside except for a little way down from the rim.

Figure 16.5   Wax resist decoration — dipping into a second glaze of contrasting colour

Figure 16.6 Thrown pot — iron and cobalt pigment over a white slip — Malcolm Pepper

Figure 16.7 Goblet with brush work decoration — Alan Caiger-Smith

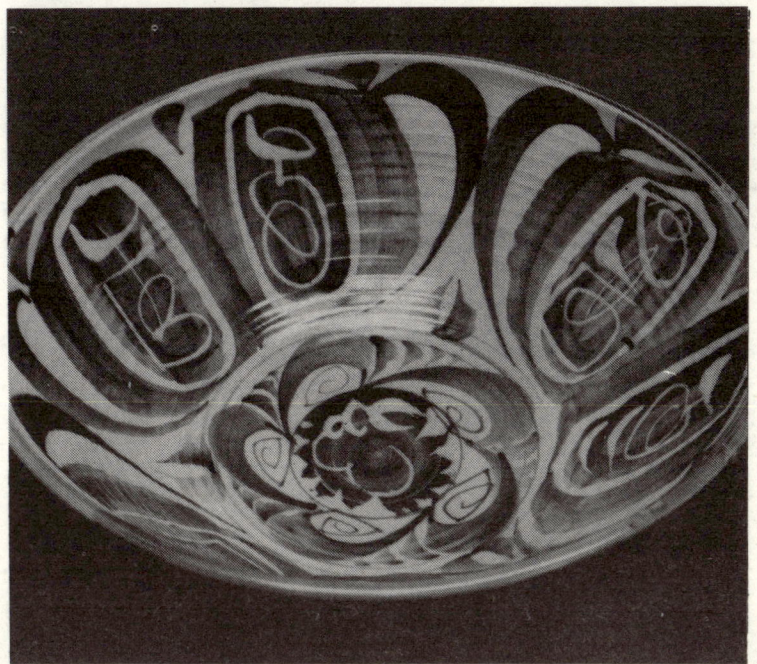

Figure 16.8 Large bowl with free brush work and wax resist — Alan Caiger-Smith (courtesy of the Hampshire Museum Service)

Figure 16.9   Small bowl, pigment banded over wax resist decoration – Bernard
Leach (courtesy of the Hampshire Museum Service)

Wax emulsions are generally available now, and these are kinder to brushes than hot, melted wax and easier to clean. Many craft potters prefer to use melted wax (usually a mixture of paraffin wax or wax candles and paraffin heated in a can on a stove) because it gives a clear, sharp image and dries very quickly on cooling. However, brushes need to be kept specially for use with hot wax, and care needs to be exercised, otherwise good-quality brushes can be ruined if the wax is too hot. Candles and wax crayons can be used on the biscuited surface to resist glaze.

Glaze~firing

Figure 17.1   Earthenware glost firing, with
Top: Slipware and agate ware
Middle: Random poured glazes and wax resist
Bottom: Ceramic pancakes and pinched owl
Note how those pieces with glaze underneath are support on
stilts

The glaze (or glost) firing is carried out when the glazed ware has
dried, and it is during this firing that the glaze materials melt and fuse.
Careful packing (figures 17.1 and 17.2) is very important because
glazed pieces must not be allowed to touch each other, and to make
the firing economical thought must be given to the use of kiln furniture. Shelves of fire-clay — known as *bats* — rest on props. Props can
be used to support the bats in either three or four places for balance,
with further props placed in the same position on the next shelf, and
so on.

Figure 17.2 Stoneware glost firing — note how a small bat is used at the top of the kiln to make economical use of kiln space

Earthenware pots, which are often left glazed underneath, need to be supported on stilts or spurs to prevent the glaze, when it matures, from causing the work to adhere to the shelf.

Stoneware and porcelain must be completely free of glaze underneath. Stilts cannot be used successfully at very high temperatures without distortion to the stilt or to the form it is supporting. Some kind of bat wash, a highly refractory material such as alumina, may be used on the shelves to prevent work from sticking as it vitrifies.

Glaze firings can be carried out quickly. After a short period on medium to get rid of water still in the work as a result of glaze application, the kiln can be bunged and switched to high. When the required temperature has been reached, the kiln is switched off and allowed to cool slowly.

Note Some glazes may require a short period of 'soaking' when the maximum temperature is maintained to help glaze maturation.

Temperatures vary according to the glazes being used: generally, 980–1150 °C for earthenware (1060 °C being the optimum for many glazes in popular use), 1250–1300 °C for stoneware and 1250–1400 °C for porcelain.

Slow cooling is important to prevent sudden thermal contraction of the glaze which will cause *crazing* (see below). The kiln must be cool before being opened, for the same reasons. The door may be eased open slowly when the temperature is down to 100 °C but it is all too easy to be impatient!

GLAZE FAULTS

Sometimes, certain imperfections will be seen on glazed work. Not all of these are considered to be wrong or undesirable in studio conditions; often, they will be seen as part of the character of handmade work, adding both visual and tactile interest. Tiny spots of iron from the clay body may speckle the glaze surface. *Pinholing*, a result of hot gases escaping or of fine particles of dust under the glaze, is quite common. However, some faults can occur which do spoil the finished work, and these can be prevented.

Crawling is the term used to describe blobs of glaze which have run away, leaving bare patches of clay. The common cause for this is dust or grease on the biscuit form, and careful storage and handling of biscuit is the remedy. *Crazing*, that is, fine cracks spreading over the glazed area, can be the result of thermal shock — the sudden contraction of the glaze if a kiln is opened too quickly, or because of a bad 'fit' of body and glaze. In the latter case, the glaze, on cooling, shrinks more than the body. *Bloating* is seen as large blisters on the surface and is usually the result of the clay body being overfired. It may be the fault of the kiln, not necessarily your tutor!

18

Ideas

USE OF NATURAL SOURCES

Much of this book has been concerned with processes and techniques and I have tried to show how each method of forming, with its own characteristics, can suggest ideas and direction. Design, therefore, can come about as a direct result of the forming process. It can also be dictated, in the case of 'useful' pottery, by function allied to aesthetic consideration. There is a great deal to be learnt by looking at the work of competent studio potters or at ceramics in art galleries and museums. But I think that it is much more valid and rewarding, if, wherever possible, you can work from your own, first-hand, experience.

Mastering technique is not such a virtue if it works only within areas of design that are derivative and secondhand, so no matter how ordinary you think your life or environment is, you can always find interesting starting points in the most common places.

Nature provides an abundance of wonderful shapes which can be put to creative use. I often feel an exciting sense of discovery when I look at something closely for the first time. There is no need to search for the rare or the exotic for inspiration. Wild plants, pebbles, seed pods, whole or sectioned fruits, shells, leaves and anything with a structure, natural or man-made, can be used to stimulate the imagination (see figure 18.6).

Some drawing can be very helpful before actually working in clay, and there is no need to worry if you think you cannot draw because it is not necessary to struggle for a representational 'likeness'. You are quite at liberty to change and transpose to suit yourself, just using the natural object as a starting point.

If you are looking at some fragment or isolated detail you should not have much trouble in making a simple sketch because, if you have not seen it before, you will not be inhibited by having to make it look 'right'. A small sketch book could well be an essential addition to your tool kit so that you can always be ready to record observations and ideas in the time between attending your course meetings.

SOME WAYS TO USE NATURAL OBJECTS

Impression
To give surface interest to clay, or to decorate a piece of work, the object, for example, a leaf, can be impressed into the clay.

Reproduction
The object can simply be made in clay, rendering it hard and permanent.

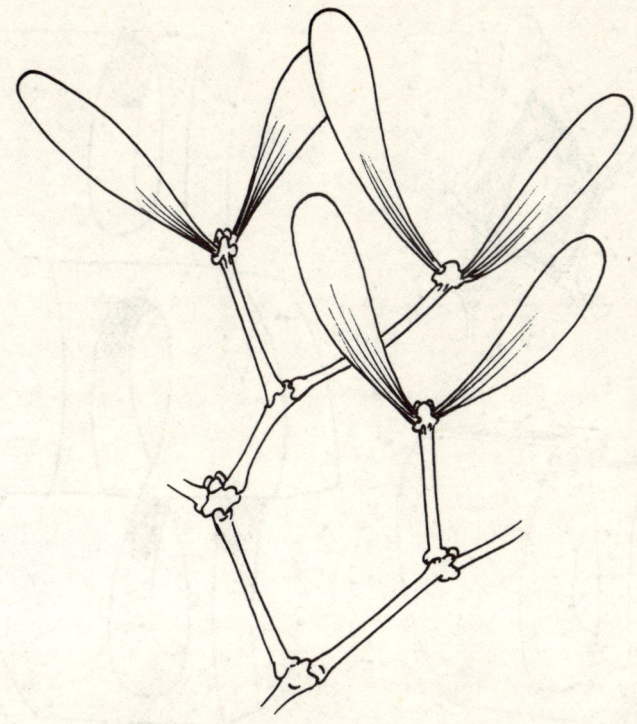

Figure 18.1   A drawing of a sprig of mistletoe

Figure 18.2   A pair of leaves, curved and simple, could be used as a decorative motif on a bowl. This could be done at any stage in the making — that is, incised or applied when the clay is workable, or brushed oxide or wax resist at the glazing stage

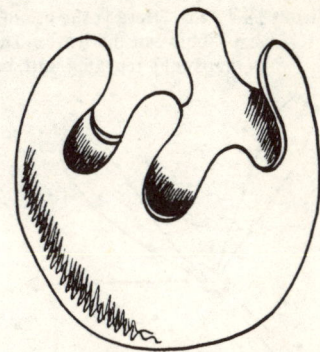

Figure 18.3   The leaves could suggest an actual form, perhaps a pinch pot with an undulating rim

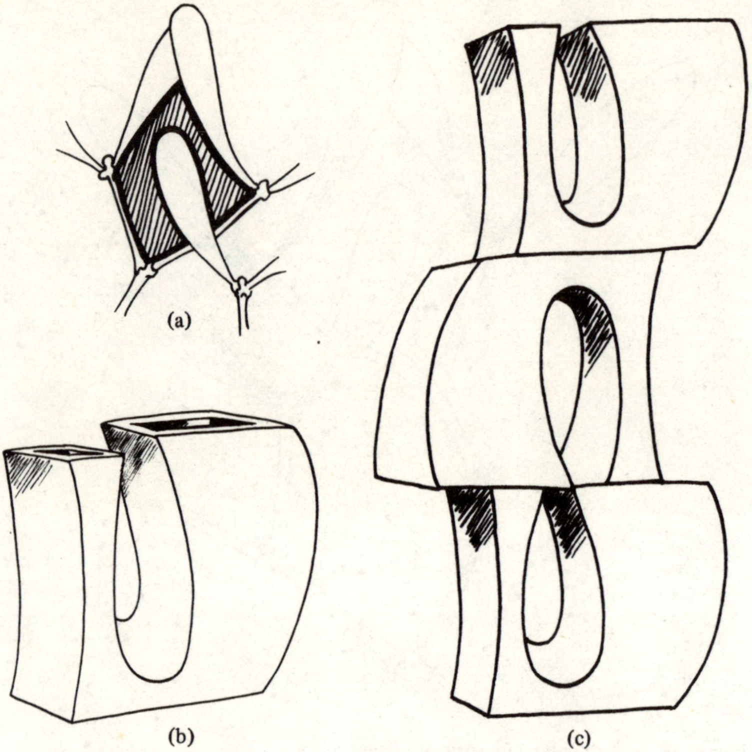

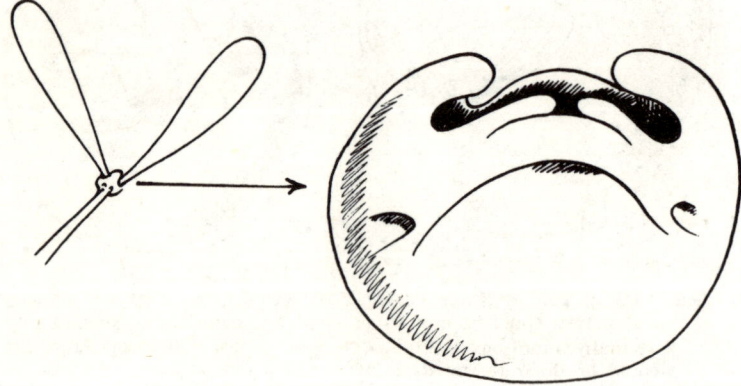

Figure 18.4 (a) Here is the use of something that is not there – the 'negative' shape between the leaves. This could take the form of (b) a slab pot or perhaps (c) a repeated unit, cut from thick slabs to build a modular form

Figure 18.5 Isolation and magnification – the join between the leaves, inverted and modified a little, could be the design for a rugged sculptural coil pot

Figure 18.6   Various ceramic forms derived from natural sources – sections of fruit, seed pods, pebbles

Figure 18.7   'Pumpkin pot', coil-built, stoneware glaze with copper oxide

Figure 18.8   Thrown, pierced bowl with 'Trees' – Alvin Betteridge

Change in Scale
Making the object smaller or larger can be interesting in itself.

Simplification
A complicated form can be simplified by using only the essential and more interesting elements of the structure. This distillation process can lead you to abstraction and invention.

Colour
A complete change from the natural colour can be interesting and amusing.

Isolation and Magnification
Close examination, perhaps through a magnifying glass or microscope, may reveal fascinating shapes with sculptural potential.

To exemplify some of these ways of using simple, natural objects to generate ideas, I have used a sprig of mistletoe, chosen for no particular reason; any found object could be used similarly (see figures 18.1 to 18.5).

Figure 18.9   Slabbed, pierced form with 'Trees' – Alvin Betteridge

19

Further ideas

It is possible to spend many years exploring particular facets of pottery. The bowl, for example, with all its subtleties in character and proportion, has, for many potters, been a source of constant interest. The very nature of the throwing technique offers an absorbing challenge which can result in total commitment to the pursuit of refinement of skill and its application. But not everyone attending pottery courses will have the desire or the resources to devote a lifetime to ceramic art, so here are a few starting points which may stimulate the imagination towards some original work.

MODULAR BUILDING
Choose a simple unit, such as a slabbed cylinder or a sphere made from two joined pinch pots. Make a number of these units and see how they can be used to develop structures. By building vertically and horizontally, you can make sculptural forms, taking into account 'visual' and 'actual' weight from all angles until you arrive at a satisfactory conclusion.

VARIATIONS ON A THEME
Using a simple unit, as above, which can be repeated, this time explore ways of making changes to the unit (figure 19.1). Working with one shape will allow ideas to be developed and modified. The variations could be concerned with any of the following examples.

Change in Scale
A 'set' of three units, changing in size, is particularly satisfying; you can refer from one to the other; they are a unified family.

Change in Surface
Try all the ways you know of changing the appearance of the form without actually altering its size or shape. Four spheres perhaps made from joined pinch pots, can have four very different characters if the surface is altered by working on it while the clay is still leather hard.

Distortion
Make changes by bending, beating, piercing and cutting a unit. For example, plain cylinders, thrown or slab-built, can be cut through and reassembled, pinched out with the fingers on the rim, or dented to affect interesting changes in the straight, regular form.

Personal Interest
Think of ways you can use clay to express your own particular interests. For example, if you enjoy gardening, you could make a

Figure 19.1 Variations on a sphere — the spheres were slip cast in the two-piece mould seen being made in chapter 8, and the variations shown here are: Top, left to right: distortion and pinching, dripped slip, 'breaking' Bottom, left to right: incising, carving and banding with cobalt and iron oxide. Note that the centre bottom sphere is biscuit fired only and has not shrunk as much as the others

Figure 19.2 'Little Ladies', press-moulded, then individually modelled; terra-cotta

Figure 19.3 'Gnome's Home', thrown in sections, pierced and modelled with wax resist and brushed oxide surface

Figure 19.4 Strange plant form, pinched with thrown stem, terracotta

Figure 19.5   Ceramic shoe, cheque book and scissors, slabbed and modelled

Figure 19.6   Surrealistic telephone, slab-built and modelled, yellow earthenware glaze — Adrian Smith

miniature watering-can or wheelbarrow. These things need not have any function or even any significance to anyone else, but they can be whimsical and personal.

Imaginative Ceramics

Imagine you have been the only visitor to another planet. You have seen things which you cannot possibly draw or describe in words; they are neither 'animal' nor 'vegetable', but completely unlike anything else you have ever experienced. Make one in clay! (See figure 19.4.)

Incongruous Objects

Think of something which, just for amusement, would be absolutely useless made in clay, for example, food: pasties, cakes and pies can be made to look very realistic. Everyday things, such as shoes and purses, can be fun to make (figure 19.5) and will test your ingenuity (and possibly your credibility!).

Ceramics need not be functional or even justifiable. Sometimes, the end result, the finished piece, may even be a little disappointing, but the initial idea and the excitement generated by that idea, followed by the creative process, the thinking, the working out and the making are all valuable experiences.

Safety and workshop practise

Ceramic materials of all kinds can be considered potentially harmful. Clay contains silica, and therefore clay itself, in the form of dust, could, over a long period of time, cause respiratory disease. Most materials are now lead free but still should be treated with care because again silica is present in glazes and many other compounds. Some oxides in themselves are toxic in their raw state and should be handled with care. In addition all equipment could be potentially dangerous.

A BRIEF GUIDE TO PROPER PROCEDURES

(1) Avoid making dust; if you have to work on dry clay, do it over a damp piece of paper so that dust and scrapings are caught and not breathed in.

(2) Avoid unnecessary handling of glaze, oxides, etc., and always replace lids on containers.

(3) Wipe up any spillage of glaze immediately, before it turns to dust.

(4) Wash down wheels, benches and boards after use.

(5) Clean all tools after use.

(6) Do not smoke in the workshop.

(7) Do not eat or drink in the workshop.

(8) Always wash your hands after handling any materials and scrub your fingernails.

(9) Clean cuts and scratches immediately and keep such wounds out of glaze.

(10) Do not open kilns unless you have permission and have checked all switches.

(11) Do not use a pug mill unless you have received permission, and instruction on its proper use.

(12) Take care when operating switches on electrical equipment, especially with wet hands.

(13) Keep plaster away from the clay area and never put clay used for plaster mould-making back into the clay bin.

Useful information: throwing weights, sizes and shrinkage rates

THROWING – WEIGHTS AND SIZES

The following is a guide to how much clay is required to make particular types and sizes of pot on a wheel. These measurements were taken immediately after throwing, so allowance should be made for shrinkage. The figures should be taken only as a guide and measurements are to the nearest 5 mm and to the nearest $\frac{1}{8}$ in. with dimensions of height followed by width.

Weight of Clay	Cylinder	Bowl
0.227 kg	80 x 70 mm small mug	50 x 110 mm
(0.5 lb)	($3\frac{1}{8}$ x $2\frac{3}{4}$ in.)	(2 x $4\frac{1}{4}$ in.)
0.340 kg	100 x 80 mm generous mug	60 x 130 mm
(0.75 lb)	(4 x $3\frac{1}{8}$ in.)	($2\frac{3}{8}$ x $5\frac{1}{8}$ in.)
0.454 kg	120 x 100 mm	65 x 150 mm cereal bowl
(1 lb)	($4\frac{3}{4}$ x $3\frac{7}{8}$ in.)	($2\frac{1}{2}$ x 6 in.)
0.907 kg	180 x 120 mm 2-pint jug	90 x 190 mm 2-pint casserole
(2 lb)	(7 x $4\frac{3}{4}$ in.)	($3\frac{1}{2}$ x $7\frac{1}{2}$ in.)
1.814 kg	255 x 130 mm	130 x 190 mm 4-pint casserole
(4 lb)	(10 x $5\frac{1}{8}$ in.)	($5\frac{1}{8}$ x $7\frac{1}{2}$ in.)
2.722 kg	300 x 130 mm	150 x 230 mm 6-pint casserole
(6 lb)	(12 x $5\frac{1}{8}$ in.)	(6 x 9 in.)

SHRINKAGE RATES

The diameter of the base of a dish, thrown from a lightly grogged body, measured the following at various stages of the ceramic process (to the nearest 5 mm and to the nearest $\frac{1}{8}$ in.).

When thrown	270 mm ($10\frac{5}{8}$ in.)
Leather hard	260 mm ($10\frac{1}{4}$ in.)
Green (dry state)	255 mm (10 in.)
Biscuit (1000 °C)	250 mm ($9\frac{7}{8}$ in.)
Stoneware (1260 °C)	240 mm ($9\frac{1}{2}$ in.)

Some ceramic materials in common use

Alumina	A refractory material naturally present in most clays. Used as a 'stiffener' in glazes to help glaze adhere to the surface of the pot during firing. Also used as a 'bat wash' to prevent work from sticking to kiln shelves
Antimony Oxide	A source of yellow **(toxic)**
Ball Clay	A plastic clay sometimes added to glazes to introduce alumina and silica
Barium Oxide and *Carbonate*	A flux used to produce matt glazes **(toxic)**
Bentonite	A very sticky clay sometimes added to clay bodies to improve plasticity. Also used to aid glaze suspension
Borax	A low temperature flux used in fritted form
Chalk	See *Whiting*
China Clay (Kaolin)	A pure clay used to introduce alumina and silica into bodies and glazes
Chromium Oxide	A source of green. Will produce pinks if used with tin oxide **(toxic)**
Cobalt Oxide and *Carbonate*	The main source of blue. Very powerful **(toxic)**
Copper Oxide and *Carbonate*	A source of green. Will produce reds in reduction firing
Cornish Stone	A granite containing a high percentage of feldspar so often used as a flux in stoneware glazes
Dolomite (Calcium Magnesium Carbonate)	A natural rock sometimes used as a flux in stoneware glazes. Also produces a semi-matt texture
Feldspar	An important and commonly used flux in stoneware glazes. Contains alumina and silica
Fireclay	A coarse-textured clay which will withstand high temperature
Flint	A source of silica in bodies and glazes
Frit	A commercially produced base glaze (earthenware) made by heating soluble fluxes with silica and then finely grinding to a powder
Grog	Ground-down, fired clay which is added to a clay body to lessen shrinkage and to coarsen the texture

Gum Arabic	Used when painting oxides or other pigments on to biscuit and fired glazed surfaces to help adhesion
Iron Oxide, Chromate and *Crocus Martis*	Sources of yellows, reds, browns and blacks (grey in reduction firing)
Lead	A low temperature flux used in fritted form *(Lead Bisilicate)*. Not always used in schools and further education establishments, but relatively safe in fritted form **(toxic)**
Limestone	See *Whiting*
Magnesium Carbonate and *Dioxide*	A high temperature flux sometimes used in stoneware glazes
Manganese Carbonate and *Dioxide*	Sources of 'purples' and browns
Nepheline Syenite	A feldspar with low temperature fluxing properties
Nickel Oxide	A source of green
Quartz	A source of silica often used in glazes as an alternative to *Flint*
Rutile	A colouring oxide containing iron and titanium, producing speckled effects
Silica	The important glass-forming material in glaze making. Introduced in the form of china clay, flint, feldspar and quartz
Sodium Oxide (Soda Ash)	A low temperature flux sometimes used in the making of frits. A deflocculant in casting slips
Sodium Silicate (Water Glass)	A deflocculant used in the preparation of casting slips
Talc (Magnesium Silicate)	A flux sometimes used as a matting agent in glazes
Tin Oxide	An opacifying oxide
Titanium Oxide	An opacifying oxide producing a semi-matt surface in glazes
Wood Ash	A source of alumina and silica which can be used in the making of stoneware glazes
Whiting (Chalk, Limestone, Calcium Carbonate)	A flux in stoneware glazes, large quantities of which will produce matt effects
Zinc Oxide	A matting agent in glazes
Zirconium	An opacifying oxide

Suggested reading

Birks, Tony, *The Art of the Modern Potter* (Country Life, Feltham, 1976).

Brears, Peter, *The English Country Pottery: Its History and Technique* (David & Charles, Newton Abbot, 1971).

Casson, Michael, *Pottery in Britain Today* (Tiranti, London, 1967).

Fraser, Harry, *Glazes for the Craft Potter* (Pitman, London, 1976).

Hamilton, David, *Manual of Pottery and Ceramics* (Thames & Hudson, London, 1974).

Jackson, Anne (ed.), *The Craft of the Potter* (BBC, London, 1977).

Leach, Bernard, *A Potter's Book* (Faber, London, 1976).

Lewenstein, Eileen, and Cooper, Emmanuel, *New Ceramics* (Studio Vista, London, 1974).

Glossary of terms

Agate Ware	Pottery made from partially mixed clays of contrasting colour, giving a marbled appearance
Ash Glaze	A glaze made wholly or partly of washed wood ash
Banding Wheel	A small turntable or whirler
Bat	A kiln shelf or a flat board for working on or carrying pots
Biscuit (Bisque)	First-fired pottery, porous and unglazed
Bloat	A blister on an over-fired form
Blunger	A machine for mixing slip
Body	The clay fabric from which a pot is made
Cast	A clay form made in a mould
Collaring	Making a narrow neck on a thrown pot by containing and reducing between the hands and fingers
Cones	Small ceramic pyramids for measuring heat/work in a kiln
Coning	Raising centred clay prior to throwing to promote mixing and to create a responsive consistency
Cottle	A wall to retain plaster when mould making
Crawling	A glaze defect — glaze running and leaving bare patches
Crazing	A glaze defect — a network of cracks as a result of glaze contraction during cooling
Deflocculant	A material added to slip to cause the clay particles to separate, so that less water is required
Dunting	Cracking of pottery by sudden thermal shock when a kiln is opened too quickly
Earthenware	Low fired, porous body. Low fired glazed pottery
Enamel	Low temperature coloured glazes applied to a glazed form and requiring a third firing
Encaustic	The technique of inlaying with slip or soft clay
Engobe	A slip; mixture of clay and water
Feathering	The technique of making delicate patterns by drawing a feather across lines of trailed slip
Fettling	Detail finishing and tidying of a form
Gallery	A ledge to support a lid
Glost	The glaze firing
Green	The dry state of clay prior to biscuit
Harp	A wire cutting tool for producing slabs of regular thickness
Kidney	A kidney-shaped smoothing tool of steel or rubber
Kneading	Rhythmic mixing of clay by hand
Knuckling Up	The technique of raising the wall of a thrown cylinder with the knuckle of the index finger
Lawn	A sieve used to prepare glaze or slip

Leather Hard	Clay which is not quite dry and still fairly workable and capable of being joined
Luting	The technique of joining clay pieces with slip
Majolica	A technique of decorating with coloured glaze on top of a tin glaze before glost firing (originally Italian pottery so decorated)
Model	An initial form from which a mould is made
Modelling	Shaping and manipulating plastic clay
Mould	A biscuit or plaster shape on, or in, which clay is formed
Natch or *Notch*	An indentation in part of a piece-mould which locates with a projection in the neighbouring piece of the mould
Oxidation	A clean, oxygen-burning firing
Oxide	Metallic substance; being a source of colour in ceramics
Paddling	A term to describe the beating of a clay form with a flat stick to achieve the desired shape
Plastic	A workable malleable clay consistency
Props	Shelf supports in a kiln
Porcelain	High fired non-porous, often translucent, body
Pug Mill	A machine for mixing clay
Pyrometer	An instrument for measuring kiln temperature
Reduction	A smoky kiln atmosphere where little oxygen is burned, its supply having been 'reduced'
Refractory	Able to resist high temperature
Rib	A tool used to shape a thrown form, often specially shaped to effect a particular finish to a rim
Saggar	A refractory clay box used in industry to protect glazed ware in a firing
Sgraffito	The technique of scratching through a surface to reveal another
Shard or *Sherd*	A fragment of broken pottery
Slake	To add an excess of water to dry clay to soften and break it up
Slip	A creamy mixture of clay and water
Slurry	A thick, lumpy mixture of clay and water
Sprigging	The technique of relief decoration with small press-moulded clay shapes
Spur	A small triangular support for glazed ware in a kiln
Stilt	A three-legged support for glazed ware in a kiln
Stoneware	High fired, non-porous body
Tenmoku	A dark brown-black iron stoneware glaze
Terracotta	An earthenware, unglazed body, usually red
Throwing	The technique of forming clay on a wheel
Trailing	The technique of drawing fluid lines of slip

Turning	The technique of shaving away excess clay from a thrown pot
Vitreous	Glass-like; non-porous
Wedging	The technique of hand mixing clay by cutting and slamming

Pottery Suppliers

WENGERS LTD, Etruria, Stoke-on-Trent. (0782 25126)

PODMORE & SONS LTD, Shelton, Stoke-on-Trent. (0782 24571)

HARRISON MAYER LTD, Meir, Stoke-on-Trent. (0782 316111)

THE FULHAM POTTERY LTD, 210 New Kings Road, London SW6 4NY. (01 736 1188)

POTCLAYS LTD, Brickiln Lane, Etruria, Stoke-on-Trent. (0782 29816)

RATCLIFFE, Rope Works, Shelton New Road, Stoke-on-Trent. (0782 611321/3)

CROMARTIE KILNS LTD, Park Hall Road, Longton, Stoke-on-Trent. (0782 313947/319435)

KILNS & FURNACES LTD, Keele Street Works, Tunstall, Stoke-on-Trent. (0782 84642)

BRIAR WHEEL & SUPPLIES, Arch Farm, Whitsbury Road, Fordingbridge, Hants. (0425 52991)

FERRO (Gt Britain) LTD, Wombourne, Wolverhampton, WV5 8DA. (Wombourne 4144)

WEBCOT, Alfred Street, Fenton, Stoke-on-Trent. (0782 45342/3)

Wilfred's White Wardrobe, slab built and modelled stoneware –
David Hamilton (courtesy of Portsmouth Museum and Art Gallery)

Chimney pots, made from two wheel-thrown sections and decorated with white 'pipe' slip – late 19th/early 20th century, Fareham, Hampshire: it is interesting to note regional variations

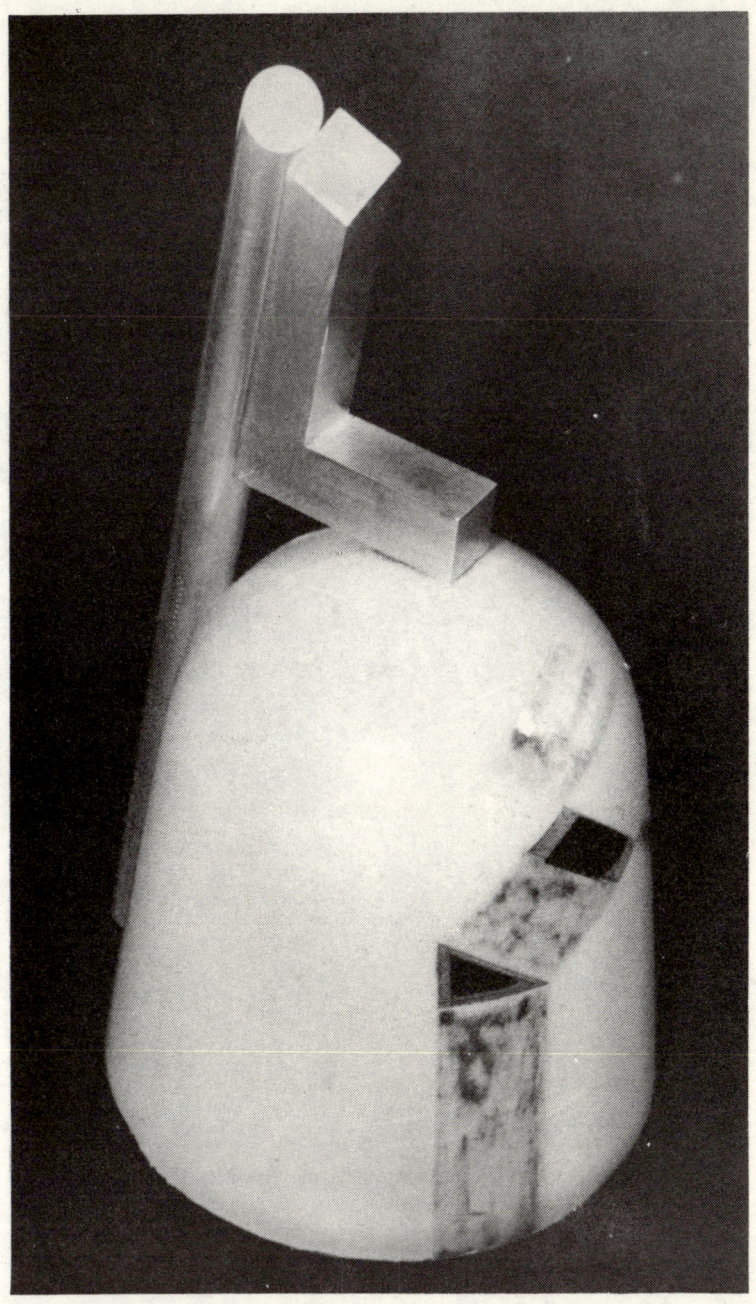

Porcelain form with underpainting, lustres and aluminium additions —
Brian Bishop, A.R.C.A. (courtesy of the artist)

Pots with inscribed words, stoneware — Ian Hamilton Finlay//Roger Bunn

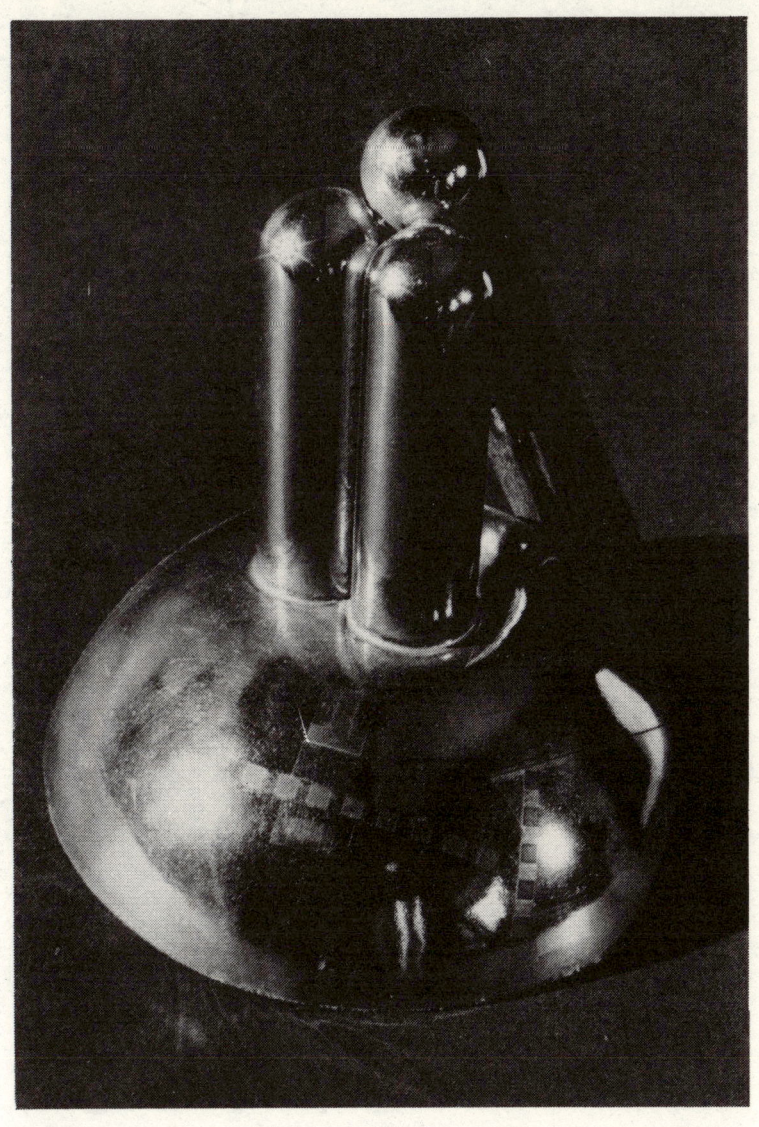

Three Verticals One Leaning, porcelain with lustres and enamels
– Brian Bishop, A.R.C.A. (courtesy of the artist)